ALSO BY A. J. MONTE AND RICK SWOPE

Take Charge of Your Money Now! Workbook

The Market Guys' Five Points for Trading Success:
Identify, Pinpoint, Strike, Protect, and Act!

Take Charge of Your Money Now!

Essential Strategies for Winning in Any Financial Climate

Take Charge of Your Money Now!

A. J. Monte *and* **Rick Swope**

BALLANTINE BOOKS

NEW YORK

Copyright © 2009 by A. J. Monte and Rick Swope

All rights reserved.

Published in the United States by Ballantine Books,
an imprint of The Random House Publishing Group,
a division of Random House, Inc., New York.

BALLANTINE and colophon are registered trademarks of Random House, Inc.

ISBN 978-0-345-51733-3

Printed in the United States of America on acid-free paper

www.ballantinebooks.com

9 8 7 6 5 4 3 2 1

FIRST EDITION

Book design by Mary A. Wirth

To the American people who have carried the torch for
  freedom throughout the world.

History shows that when faced with a challenge you will overcome.

You feed the hungry and clothe the naked.

When disasters strike and people fall, you come to the rescue.

You defend the oppressed and helpless.

Your ingenuity, tenacity, and leadership are to be admired.

Your critics persist in their attempt to strike you down
  as you fight their battles.

Stay alert, stand united, and be good stewards of your wealth.

It is not greed that dictates what we do with our fortunes,

But divine providence revealing to us that wealth has a purpose.

May we use our wealth to change the world for the better,

And leave a legacy in the process.

Contents

INTRODUCTION xi

PART 1. THE GAME 1

 Chapter 1. Know the Market 3
 Chapter 2. Speak the Language of the Market 9
 Chapter 3. Choosing Your Market 20

PART 2. THE PLAYERS 33

 Chapter 4. Know Yourself 35
 Chapter 5. Who's Watching Your Money? 47
 Chapter 6. If You're Not Angry, You're Not Paying Attention 74

PART 3. THE STRATEGY 99

 Chapter 7. Create a Family Budget 101
 Chapter 8. Keep It Super Simple 111
 Chapter 9. Secrets of the Marketplace 119
 Chapter 10. Invest without Fear 130

PART 4. THE PURPOSE 139

 Chapter 11. The Threat of Complacency 141
 Chapter 12. What Is Your Purpose? 145

PART 5. THE UNEXPECTED   153

   Chapter 13. Taking Charge of the Unexpected   155

          Bankruptcy   157

          Catastrophic Expenses   163

          College Students   167

          Divorce   170

          Foreclosure   174

          Identity Theft   178

          Job Loss   181

          Marriage   185

          Retirement   189

          Starting a Family   193

          Windfalls   197

ACKNOWLEDGMENTS   203

INDEX   205

Introduction

Taking charge of your money is the first step toward taking charge of your life. No man has ever had his personal house in order whose financial house is in disarray.

Why Bother with Another Money Book?

In our first book, *The Market Guys' Five Points for Trading Success*, we included a question that is often asked of us by people who have yet to hear us speak: "Why should I listen to anything you have to tell me?" It's a fair question. You have every right to question the authority and credentials of someone who offers you their advice. You well know that there are many gurus and experts out there propounding their philosophies of health, wealth, and happiness. The philosophies, ideas, and strategies range from bizarre to inspirational. So how do you decide between sound advice and nonsense?

To help you answer the question we just posed, it might be useful to plant another question in your mind. You are holding in your hand a book about taking charge of your money—and doing it now. Maybe you've gotten to this point without asking yourself this question: With the many hundreds of books published about money and personal finance, why bother with yet another money book? There are three key reasons why we're confident this book will help you take charge of your money.

1. Wall Street and Main Street

We bring the lessons and insights of the world of professional trading and investing to the everyday needs and challenges of Main Street. You have to be in the markets to really understand how they work. You can't simply read about the trading floor in New York or listen to the news reports on the financial networks. You have to put your own money at risk and know what it feels like to make a profit and suffer a loss. Have you made a great money decision and felt the excitement of winning? Or have you made a serious error and lain awake all night wondering how you'll recover? Very few people get that opportunity, and even fewer are willing or able to take that experience and extend it to real-life financial issues. We have been in the trenches of Wall Street and know how the financial world operates. We've seen what it takes to win and what happens when you lose. We didn't create The Market Guys as a marketing brand to make money in the world of business advice. The Market Guys brand grew out of our understanding and passion for the markets and investing. Along the way, we realized that professional trading and investing principles can be applied to personal finance with great success. Key lessons that every Wall Street professional knows are brought to you in this book to help you manage your money like the pros.

2. Practical, Time-Tested Strategies

Gimmicks may sound great in advertising, but they rarely stand the test of time. Through our many years in the financial business, we have had the privilege of working with millions of traders and investors around the world. We have seen the practices and habits of people who are successful with their money, and we have seen other practices and habits that are common to the unsuccessful people. This book brings our years of accumulated observations and experiences to you in an easy-to-follow format. We're not developing a theory of finance here; many others have traveled that road before us. What we're offering in this book is a map—a practical, useful guide to getting to your destination, regardless of your starting point. If you diligently follow the map, you can achieve success with your finances and take charge of your money!

One of the reasons we're so excited about offering you this book is that we are in front of audiences around the world every day, and we get their feedback. We know that the strategies and ideas contained in the pages that follow have already changed lives for the better. We've heard about the people who have taken charge of their money, and their stories inspire us. We want you to be one of those success stories. If you choose to act, you can do it!

3. Protect and Grow

The basic tenet of our approach to taking charge of your money is to manage risk first and then build from there. We are not part of the hype that tells you that the stock market is your own personal lottery ticket. We're not going to try to convince you that you can buy and sell houses the way kids trade baseball cards. We know that if something smells fishy, it's probably because it contains a rotten fish. We'll talk to you about the fact that every professional knows you can't grow your money if you don't take care to protect it. The next goal, then, is to learn key strategies to help you grow your wealth in small, steady steps. This book isn't about spinning the roulette wheel and hoping you land the big payoff. We're offering you real meat-and-potatoes ideas, not long shots. If you've been looking for a money book that you can use as a how-to manual rather than a wish-I-could book, then keep reading.

How Do You Use This Book?

We wanted this book to be practical and usable right from the start. Sometimes you have to labor all the way through a book before you can piece together the ideas and put them to work. Other times, the themes are so arcane or pie-in-the-sky that even after you're done with the book, you're left wondering how it could possibly apply to your situation. Our goal was to avoid both of these traps.

We have structured the book into four major sections. The first is all about markets. We start with the premise that you really need to understand whatever market you're participating in. If you're investing in the stock market, you need to know how stock markets work and how to avoid the traps and dangers. Along with that, each market has its own language and we talk about why it's crucial that you learn to communicate in that specific language.

The second section deals with the players—what people and institutions make up your market? The first player, of course, is you. We deal with some of the considerations that make you the best market player you can be. Beyond that, we talk about friends and foes within your market. This includes how to pick your friends, such as your financial advisor and broker. We also deal very strongly with your foes—those people and companies that are actively trying to harm you as a by-product of their own selfish interests. We make it a point to say, "If you're not angry, you're not paying attention!"

The third section is concerned with your strategy. Now that you understand the markets and who the players are, how can you be most effective within that market? We introduce you to what you need for creating a financial plan and how to put your internal motivation to work for you.

Finally, we've included a section on special circumstances. It would be great if life followed a prescribed set of rules and you knew what was coming next. That's not life; the unexpected is always lurking right around the corner. We've included many of the common special issues that you may encounter including divorce, foreclosure, and bankruptcy.

The chapters are designed as stand-alone nuggets. If you read only the first couple of chapters or you decide to jump ahead to the chapter on unexpected circumstances, you'll be armed with useful information that you can use today.

Our *Take Charge of Your Money Now! Workbook* is designed to make sure that you know and understand the key ideas. Again, this isn't a test that must be completed in sequence. Jump around, find the parts that interest you, and then come back to the rest of the book later. Even better, take copious notes on the section that applies to you, and create your own personal reference manual. Use your own notes to teach someone else—your kids or grandkids, for example—and you'll find that you become a better student and teacher at the same time!

Why Now?

You might be thinking that all of this sounds good so far, but what's the urgency? You agree that you need to take charge of your money, but maybe later, not now. As we complete the manuscript for this book at the end of 2008, the financial world is being rocked. We're watching events and changes that haven't been seen in generations, if ever. Consider some of the momentous events of 2008:

- Investor fraud worth $50 billion was perpetrated by a single money manager.
- Oil prices ran to an all-time high of over $140 a barrel, and then dropped $100 within six months.
- Christmas retail sales were the worst in forty years.
- The Consumer Confidence Index dropped to the lowest point since its 1967 inception.
- Unemployment reached a fifteen-year high and was expected to continue to rise.
- The Dow Jones Industrial Average lost almost 40 percent in 2008—the biggest one-year drop since the Great Depression.
- Titans of the banking, insurance, and manufacturing industries failed at a record pace, setting the stage for massive government bailout packages.

We don't want to frighten you with these statistics. In fact, you're quite likely already aware of everything that we've mentioned. These events should awaken within you an urgency to act. Now is not the time to be complacent or lazy. You have already taken the first step by purchasing this book. Now you need to learn the key principles for taking charge of your money. Turbulent times sort the winners from the losers. They are the winds that separate the wheat from the chaff. You can ignore these changes and take your chances on being a victim, or you can grab the reins and take charge now.

Be a winner!

Take charge of your money!

Do it now!

PART ONE

The Game

Chapter 1
Know the Market

*There are no professional traders. There are, however,
professional gold traders, professional options traders,
and professional futures traders. Every professional knows
his market—you need to know yours.*

Have you ever opened your 401(k) statement and felt sick to your stomach? Have you and your spouse had that hard conversation about whether or not you'll ever be able to retire? Do you always buy at the top of the market and sell at the bottom? Are you concerned about the cost of college tuition and how you'll pay for it with your savings? If these questions sound familiar, then you're in good company with the vast majority of the population. You have every good intention of saving for a rainy day only to find out that it looks awfully wet outside today. That leads to the obvious question: Do you stand any chance of getting out from under the control of Wall Street and actually building your savings and investments on Main Street? The answer is a resounding "Yes!"

Lest you think that mere resolve will let you march down Wall Street and take control of your financial destiny, recognize that you need to prepare yourself to change your financial future. The first step in this process is understanding the game you're playing. You might think that's an impossible task as you watch the financial shows on TV. Just about the time you realize that they really are speaking English, you're bombarded with terms like *liquidity, advancing issues,* and *credit spread.* And your best guess about the meaning of the last term is that you can't pay cash for your peanut butter.

Chances are, you've probably never had the opportunity to walk onto the floor of the New York Stock Exchange. You probably do have a picture in your mind of the screaming traders running around, clutching phones in one hand and waving stacks of notes in the other. At the same time, you're trying desperately to believe that this modern-day goat rodeo isn't the foundation on which our economy has been built. Surely there are real traders in a room somewhere who really keep things together. And if not, then how in the world do you, the hardworking investor from Main Street, stand a chance in this circus? More to the point, if the players in this game have a somewhat less altruistic motive than making sure your money is handled with care, what do you need to do to win at this game?

The Market

Let's start with the basics. When you take your money to the bank or to your broker, it eventually ends up in the market. Even if you don't buy stocks, there are money markets that pay you interest every month. However, that retirement account, college savings account, or annuity most likely includes some stocks or mutual funds. Mutual funds are nothing more than a collection of stocks and other investments that are bought and sold by the fund manager. Basically, you give the fund manager your money, and he or she decides what to buy and sell for you. When these stocks are bought and sold, the transactions are done through the stock market. The stock market is the gathering place (either real or electronic) where buyers go to find sellers and sellers go to find buyers—a sort of financial matchmaker. At the heart of the chaos that you see in the images of the trading floor is the constant pairing of buyers and sellers. Since nobody is forced to trade with anyone else, buyers and sellers have to adjust their prices to meet the demands of the other. When big news comes out, such as an announcement from the Federal Reserve (which sets interest rates), buyers and sellers scramble to adjust their prices and make their trades as quickly as possible. This creates the scenes of markets that are typically shown on news programs.

To better explain this, let's tone the picture down a few notches. Even if you've never been to an art auction, you're probably somewhat familiar with them. The auctioneer puts up an item for sale with the goal of maximizing the sale price. He watches as the buyers raise their paddles to bid on the item. At first, the paddles pop up frequently as buyers try to pick up a bargain. Throughout the proceedings, the auctioneer continues to step up the price to draw the buyers to bid as high as possible. Eventually, the number of paddles being raised ebbs with each successive rise in price, and the price increase slows down. Good auctioneers take it right up to the last buyer before dropping the gavel and declaring a sale.

The stock market is often referred to as an *auction market*. On the floor of the stock exchange, traders are looking to get the highest price from the buyers. At the same time, buyers are searching for opportunities to trade at the lowest price. Sometimes there are many more buyers than sellers, and a bidding war starts. This is what happens when a fine piece of artwork is offered by the auctioneer and the paddles pop up all over the room. Occasionally, the buyers become so intent on buying the item that they apparently throw all reason out the window as the price reaches an inexplicably high level. If you were standing at the back of the room watching this unfold, you would be hard-pressed to explain why the buyers were driving the price to such an unreasonably high level. When this happens in the stock market, it is sometimes called *irrational exuberance*.

But the wave can flow the other way, too. You've heard it said that fear and greed drive the stock market. Which of the two do you think is more powerful? Without question, fear is the more powerful emotion. Nobody wants to be left holding the bag when everyone else has made a beeline for the door. Let's shift our auction analogy a bit by imagining that you have a piece of artwork to sell. Your money is tied up in this item, and the only way you can get the necessary cash is to sell it. So you walk into the auction hall and you're met by a line of sellers, each of whom is holding his or her own item for sale. Worse yet, there are only a few buyers scattered about the hall with their paddles in hand. As you watch the sale begin, you start to get that hollow feeling in your stomach that comes with the realization that you're not going to sell your item for anywhere near what you believe it's worth. In fact, it is quite likely that you will have to practically give it away in order to extract any value. When the auctioneer finally places your item up for bid, no paddles are raised to meet the initial price. So he drops the price. And then he drops it again, hoping to entice just one buyer into the trade. You have the option of taking your item back and walking away without a sale, but you're driven by the fear that you might never be able to sell it. So you take an exceptionally low price and leave with a mere fraction of what you had expected.

At this point, you may have already forgotten that we were talking about a hypothetical art sale as your mind wandered to your retirement savings account. You see, markets are collections of individuals representing either themselves or the institutions that employ them. The point to remember is that people drive the markets, and emotions drive the people. This is no different from the way things work at an art auction, at a weekend flea market, or with an eBay listing. If the buyers are motivated, prices will rise. If the sellers are fearful and aggressive, prices will collapse. And often reason goes out the window as buyers and sellers try to close a deal before, in their minds, it's too late.

Many well-educated and informed traders and investors have tried to apply logic and programming to the markets in order to outsmart the masses. For a while they might meet with some success.

You have most likely read or heard about some of the "can't-miss" how-to systems that let you use the stock market as your own personal financial concierge. All you have to do is follow the plan, and you'll be writing checks from the market, guaranteed! But these systems assume that you can accurately predict the behavior of the people who are buying and selling. Don't kid yourself. You can no more predict the future in the stock market than you can know exactly what your five-year-old granddaughter will be doing later in the day. It all depends on how long she slept, what she ate for lunch, and whether she found your stash of chocolate in the pantry.

We once worked with a trader who carefully scoured stock price history and "discovered" a stock that went up in price at the same time every year. So he bought the stock and waited to harvest his profits. But this time the stock price dropped. So he did what most investors do when the price drops: He bought more. Then the price dropped again, and he took the cash he had left and bought even more. Eventually, the price dropped further, and fear gripped him as he watched the value of his savings dwindle. As a result of this fear, he sold everything. You see, he forgot the basics of the game he was playing. He was the only paddle in the room while the sellers were lined up with the auctioneer. After he bought the first time, the next seller stepped up, and he put his paddle up again, hoping this would make the sellers go away. Instead of retreating, the sellers kept selling until he no longer had the means to raise his paddle. Then he walked to the front of the room and joined the line of sellers. It doesn't really make much sense when you look at it this way, does it?

You Can Take Charge!

Now are you ready for the good news? You don't have to invest at the mercy of Wall Street any longer. You can take control of your finances and your future by committing right now to learning the basics of the game that you're playing. Hear what we're saying: You don't have to become a market guru. You just have to know the simple rules and how to play, and you can win! How can we say this with such unwavering confidence? Because we have worked with millions of investors all over the world, and we have seen what it takes to be successful. We have also recognized the pitfalls to avoid that lead to failure.

Here's what you need to do to get started. Grab all of your statements from your bank and broker. Lay them out on the table before you, and figure out which game you're playing. If you own stocks and mutual funds, then you're in the stock market whether you realize it or not. If your money is in a cash account, then you're on the sidelines, but you can play anytime. Dig out the stock certificates you have in your drawer, request an itemization of your investments in your company 401(k), and gather the bank statements that are still sealed in the envelopes on your counter. Maybe you don't have any extra money and you're living week to week. That's okay, because you have time to prepare and learn before you buy and sell. The key here is that you can't plot a course if you don't know where you're starting from. Rome wasn't built in a day—but eventually it was built into a great empire. Regardless of how you started, you can still finish strong!

Chapter 2

Speak the Language of the Market

The locals always get the best deals in the street markets because they know the language and customs. If you want to get the best deals in the stock market, you need to learn the language.

Now that you have an understanding of the way an auction market works in terms of stocks and mutual funds, expand your thinking into other markets about which you have an understanding or with which you have experience. Whether it be real estate, collectible coins, antique cars, or the stock market, each of these areas requires a certain level of knowledge before you should even think about investing any time or money.

Learn the Language

A good way to approach these types of investments is to think of them as though you were learning a new language. It isn't reasonable to walk around a foreign country and expect to converse with the locals if you've never studied their language. When you begin to learn any language, you start out by learning a few words at a time. As you put these words together, you develop phrases, which eventually lead to sentences. Over time, you can carry on an entire conversation as you learn the nuances of the language and how to effectively communicate.

People ask us how long it takes to learn about the markets. Consider how long it might take to learn a new language. There are several key factors that dictate the length of the learning curve. One of the factors is your capacity to learn a new language. Some people are just better at learning languages than others. Also, the amount of time you spend in study and practice has a big effect on your learning pace. Finally, when you speak the language with others who are more proficient, you decrease your learning time. Don't get frustrated and give up. The time you invest in this part of your quest to take charge of your money will pay great dividends.

Confidence Is Profitable

One of the most interesting things we have found over the years is that there is a direct correlation between investor confidence and investor profits. The more confident you are, the greater the chance you will see higher yields down the road. The opposite is also true. Less confidence in your abilities usually translates into lower profits—or even losses. You may have heard the old saying "Scared money never wins." If you want to be a winner, be sure you are doing what you can to build your confidence level each and every day. Confidence is built through study and application. First, learn to speak the language; then, as you gain confidence speaking this new language, you can go out into the world and use it.

More Markets

If you looked up the definition of *market* in a dictionary, you would see that a market is an open place or a covered building where buyers and sellers convene for the sale of goods—an example is a farmer's market. But to break it down into its simplest form, a market is any place where you would see a financial transaction being made. It could be over the counter at a supermarket; on the Internet, where people are buying and selling on eBay; or in an office, where two people are transferring ownership of a piece of property. All of these are considered markets.

For a market to function properly, at least two parties must be involved: a buyer and a seller. A purchase, a transaction, or a trade is made when the buyer and seller agree on a price at which each party perceives value. Using legal terminology, this exchange of value is called *consideration*. Most transactions we make involve money that is given in return for a promise of value or an asset.

If we are exchanging money for a home or a parcel of land, then we are participating in the real estate market. If we are buying or selling on eBay, then we are involved in an auction market. If we are buying and selling stocks, then we are most definitely trading in the stock market. You might be surprised to find out just how few people know about the stock market and how it works. So as you can see, before you even think about investing in any of these markets, it would be wise to prepare yourself, just as you are doing now by reading this book.

Education Is Risk Free

Education is a risk-free investment, and the time you put into your studies will increase the return on your investment. Be sure to put time aside every week to study. Pace yourself by taking fifteen minutes each day to read an article published in a respectable financial magazine like *Forbes* or subscribe to a publication like *Investor's Business Daily.* We also recommend that you take some time to watch a financial program on TV every now and then. However, we don't advise you to follow the recommendations of every financial expert you see on television.

The goal is for you to get a grasp of the language so you are more comfortable with the concepts behind investing. If you hear terms you are not familiar with, write them down and research them. Perhaps someone has told you that value investing is the art of buying low and selling lower—at least that's one interpretation of this strategy. However, with a little probing you will learn that value investing is a strategy that involves buying the stocks of companies that are perceived to be undervalued with the goal of holding them as a long-term investment. What you might not know is that this strategy requires you, the investor, to develop sound risk management skills to enable you to limit losses from your account.

Yahoo!

A good example of why you should understand the risks before you invest comes from an investor we dealt with in the mid-1990s. Diane had suddenly lost her husband to a heart attack and was forced to sell the store they had together owned in New York. She decided to use some of the proceeds to pay off the mortgage on her house. Although Diane had a basic understanding of how the stock market worked, she had little practical experience. Nevertheless, she decided to take $200,000 of her money and buy stock in a company she knew little about. The one thing she was certain of was that she was in love with this company's product.

The product was a chocolate drink that her grandchildren would ask for, and she remembered her favorite baseball hero, Yogi Berra, loving it, too. So one day she called up her broker and asked him to buy as many shares as he could with her $200,000. When she got her account statement the next month, she almost fell off her chair: Her account was up by more than $50,000. Excited but curious, she tried calling her broker to see what was going on with this company, but he was out of the office. Later that afternoon, her broker called her back to tell her that he had some good news and some bad news. The bad news was that she did not buy the shares she thought she had bought. There had been a mistake in the original order. The good news was that she had bought shares in Yahoo! and not Yoo-hoo, her favorite bottled beverage. Diane decided to hold on to her newfound charm of a stock and told her broker to leave things the way they were in the account.

Diane continued to profit over time, as the stock price kept climbing. She saw the stock go from $100 a share to $200 a share. Then it went through a *stock split,* which is when the company's existing shares are divided into multiple shares. This increased the number of shares she owned—after the split, she was making twice as much for every dollar the stock increased in price.

Needless to say, Diane was in heaven. When we began working with her shortly afterward, she would call us every other day to check her current account balance. Each time we spoke with her we suggested that she start moving out of this stock to lock in and protect her profits. By this time she had owned shares in Yahoo! for about three years. The stock had gone through a series of splits, leaving her with a profit of over $23 million—hard to believe, but true.

The sad part is that Diane never took her money out of that account, nor did she do anything to protect her profits. In other words, she didn't understand how risk management principles worked, and she did not take the advice of those who knew better. She thought these profits would just continue to grow for as long as she stayed invested in this company.

The beginning of the end of this story came when Diane told us that she would be going on a long cruise. She wanted to take some of her great fortune and live a little. On her cruise she went, without a care in the world, leaving her cell phone and computer behind. She didn't listen to the radio, nor did she watch any television while she was on the cruise. She just wanted to be with her friends and relax. However, there was one thing Diane forgot to do: She did not give anyone power of attorney over her account while she was away. During her vacation, the market took an unfortunate turn for the worse, and the price of the stock to which Diane was so attached went tumbling down.

When she finally got back to the United States, she checked in to see what was going on with her stock, only to find that she had lost more than 50 percent of the value of her account. She again was advised to take the remaining $11 million out of that one position in order to protect it. Once again, she ignored good advice. Instead, she decided to hold on—she believed it would all get better again and she would see that $23 million back in her account. Basically, Diane followed what we call the "ostrich strategy," which is nothing more than putting your head in the sand and hoping your problems go away.

Things went from bad to worse when Diane decided to mortgage the balance of her account to buy real estate in Boca Raton, Florida. This was another unfamiliar market for her, and ultimately poor Diane made the biggest mistake of her life. She watched in dismay as the value of both the stock and the property she owned continued to drop, leaving her in a leveraged (borrowing) position that almost crippled her financially.

This sad story shows you just how important it is to learn the language of the markets. Regardless of the market you choose, if you are looking for a return on your investment you will most likely be putting your money at risk. Every reward involves some sort of risk, but understanding risk is just the first part of the equation. The second and most important part is learning how to limit or mitigate that risk.

We interweave the concepts that underlie proper risk management strategies throughout this book. Until we get to those ideas, please don't let Diane's story scare you out of the investment world. Your confidence in your own abilities is one of the keys to your success. Many people who have followed our guidelines have seen enormous profits over the years, and there is no reason you should not join this group.

Here are three key points we can take from Diane's experience:

1. *Learn about the market you are investing in.* Make sure you are aware of things that might affect the price of the

asset you buy. Stay on top of that market, and don't just assume that things will continue to go your way.

2. *Heed the advice of experts who are trying to help you protect your assets.* Many experts want to impress you with their expertise. If you find a professional who prides herself on preserving capital, then pay careful attention to her. Chances are, she is right, and you don't want to miss an opportunity to protect your wealth.

3. *Don't use the ostrich strategy to manage your money.* Burying your head in the sand doesn't make your problem go away. Don't allow the problem to get out of your sight and then out of your mind. This is actually one of the biggest mistakes people make in their financial lives, and the basis for it is greed. Diane believed it was better to risk the $11 million she had left when she got back from her cruise in the hope that her account would return to the $23 million mark. She ignored the advice of the experts who knew better, and the decisions she made wound up costing her the entire fortune.

It seems that for every tragic story we have at least two inspirational ones. It might be because we are the ultimate optimists who are forever searching for the rainbow after the rainstorm, or it might be that more people are willing to expose their successes to us than their failures. Whatever the reason, it's always nice to deliver some good news with the bad.

Dan Takes Charge

One of the most positive stories we know comes from a gentleman named Dan. A housepainter in the Washington, D.C., area, Dan had worked hard to save a little over $2,000 in his bank account. His dream was to buy his own home without having a mortgage. So one day Dan walked into the office of a very well respected brokerage firm and asked the person behind the desk if he could speak with someone who could help him invest his money. The representative of this firm, who was also a licensed stockbroker, asked Dan how much money he had to invest. Dan told his story about how hard he had worked to save and shared his dream of being a homeowner. Dan then handed him his check to show that he was serious.

What happened next is what disturbed us the most. After Dan had confided his dream, the broker looked at the check and laughed. He said, "Sir, you would have a better chance taking this money to Las Vegas and playing the casinos, and you will most certainly have a better time losing it."

Dan was as stunned as he was infuriated. How dare this person try to rob him of the American dream? This experience motivated Dan to do it on his own without the help of any broker.

Shortly after this experience we ran into Dan at one of our seminars in Washington, D.C. He had made the decision to enroll himself in as many seminars as he could in order to learn the language that would help him reach his financial goals. There was something about Dan that interested us. He was approaching fifty years of age, and he was a man with a mission. He had his sights set on owning his own home, and there was nothing that was going to keep him from reaching that goal. When we saw this, we decided to do what we could to help Dan realize his dream.

We told him that in order to create wealth he would first have to commit time to studying the markets, which he did. We brought him along one step at a time, teaching him the difference between *bull markets* (markets controlled by buyers) and *bear markets* (markets controlled by sellers). Then we made sure Dan understood the importance of buying with the buyers and selling with the sellers. Once he learned the proper way to protect himself, we turned him loose. Month after month, Dan was able to take profits from his account. In the first month of his success, he took some of his profits and bought a small piece of land. We asked him why he had done this, and his answer was simple: "Each month I am going to take a little out of my account and use it to build my house one step at a time. Then I won't have to worry about borrowing from my bank, and I will be mortgage free when I am done."

This was an intriguing plan, and it seemed to work very well for Dan. The most important aspect of this plan was that it taught him how to protect his investment along the way. You see, he avoided the position Diane had put herself in when she failed to protect her assets. Dan knew that the only way he could build his home was to make sure he kept himself in a profitable situation and did not allow himself to fall backward. In doing this, he stayed totally committed to protecting those profits.

Each month Dan would invest in a stock that was moving up, and each month his simple plan was to take profits out of his account. He laid the foundation for his home one month, and then he went back to studying ways to profit in the market. All the while he continued to work as a housepainter. On his lunch breaks, he would call us with questions, and month after month he was able to build profits.

His $2,000 account grew to $50,000 in the first year. Six months after that we got the call from Dan telling us that he was ready to put the front door on his new home. It was a big oak door with elaborate carvings and a beautiful pattern in the middle. You could hear the emotion in his voice as he was finally realizing what the American dream is all about: freedom of choice and opportunity. This dream means people have access to great financial opportunity regardless of their race, creed, or gender. The dream is available to anyone who possesses the will and desire to learn and to those who believe in themselves enough to take charge of their money, refusing to listen to a skeptical world about their chances of success.

Dan's is one of the true success stories to which everyone can relate. He ended his story with a powerful punctuation mark: He went to the local Mercedes-Benz dealer and picked out the dream car that would grace the garage of his new home, and he paid for this car with cash. On his way home, he decided to pay a visit to that brokerage firm he had called on two years earlier.

He parked his brand-new, shiny black luxury car right at the front door of the office, strutting in as if he were a rock star. Making sure that everyone there saw him, he walked up to the front counter, looked right into the eyes of the broker who had laughed at him, and said, "You really need to find another line of work because you, my friend, are a dream stealer."

He walked out, got into his car, and drove away, knowing that the man behind the counter had given up a very profitable account— not only had Dan made enough money to build his dream home, but he also had parlayed his account to just over $1 million. Dan's story is unique since he traded stock options, which are a leveraged investment. Buying and selling stock options multiplies profits much faster than buying and selling stocks (although losses can multiply faster if you're wrong!). Nevertheless, Dan was successful because he learned the language of the markets.

The points we take from Dan's story are simple:

1. *Don't let anyone steal your dream.*
2. *Make sure you set aside time to study:*
   Education is a risk-free investment.
3. *Build and protect along the way:*
   As you realize profits, be sure to protect them.

Before we end this chapter, it's important for you to recognize that it's not just about making money. Once you learn how to overcome the obstacles that get in the way of your success, anything is possible. That is the absolute truth. We don't know how you measure up in your level of confidence, nor do we know what kind of challenges you have faced. However, we do know that everyone has faced some sort of challenge in life.

You might be someone who has already overcome those challenges and acquired all that life has to offer, so that now you are looking for tips to help you fine-tune your financial condition. You might be someone who has yet to realize that golden opportunity. The fact is, you are the only one who can make the decision to change your life for the better. You have the ability to succeed at each and every stage of your life. You merely have to realize it, and then take that first step! As The Market Guys, we have almost fifty years of combined experience in the markets, and we have a passion to help you.

Chapter 3
Choosing Your Market

The best kite won't fly on a calm day. On the other hand, a strong wind will lift even the flimsiest of kites. Investing is like flying a kite; choosing your kite is important, but you still need the power of the wind.

Thanks to the advancement in market technology, investing has never been easier. For better or worse, investors are faced with having more investment choices than at any other time in history. Whether you are a seasoned investor or a novice in the markets, it's important to understand the areas in which you plan to invest before you put your money at risk. Becoming familiar with these markets not only helps you increase your level of confidence but also helps you do a better job of managing risk. People who have greater confidence in their own abilities generally do better than those with a lower confidence level.

Stocks, or equity shares, are what we are exposed to most often when we tune in to the prime-time financial programs on most business channels. Yet if you take a finance or economics course in high school or college, you will be taught practically nothing about stocks. And investing and risk management courses are hard to find. Investing is hardly ever mentioned at the elementary or middle school level because most teachers don't have sufficient confidence in their own investing and market skills to instruct others. Further-

more, there is no incentive for including the subject in the elementary curriculum because the standardized tests at that level don't
have a section on money and personal finance. This has resulted in
generations of children who have learned what they can about financial matters from their parents. The problem is, many parents
also lack the investing skills and confidence in the markets to teach
kids what they need to know. The last thing we want is the credit
card companies teaching our kids how to invest. You see, the credit
card companies will condition your children to live beyond their
means and accept debt and interest expense as a normal part of life.
Think about the gift you'll give the next generation when you take
charge of your money and show your children how to do the same
without making all of the same mistakes.

If you would like to teach the children in your family about investing, then you might consider having them start a stamp or coin
collection. Each stamp and coin has a face value, and they can be
traded or sold on the open market the way stock certificates are.
Any stamp collector who has been in the business for a while will
tell you that each stamp has a history. The history, along with the
number of similar stamps in circulation in the open market, determines how much that stamp is worth. Buyers and sellers of stamps
are just like buyers and sellers of stocks. When the buyers are aggressively buying a particular stamp, the price of that stamp rises
dramatically. The same thing happens in the stock market. As you
discuss these scenarios, you'll find ways to communicate the important aspects of investing.

The Initial Public Offering (IPO)

An *initial public offering* is when a company issues common stock
or shares to the public for the first time. Companies that do this are
usually young, smaller companies or larger, privately owned companies that are seeking capital to expand their business. To assist
them in this process, these companies seek the help of an under-

writing firm that determines the type of security to issue—typically, either common stock or preferred stock.

Common stock, as the name implies, is the most common form of stock issued by a company. When you own common stock, you own a small part of the company represented by the stock. Common stock comes with voting rights, so you have a voice in some aspects of the business. You may also receive a *dividend,* or earning payment, from your ownership. *Preferred stock* is similar to common stock except that it usually pays a fixed dividend rather than a dividend based on company performance. Also, if the company should experience financial difficulties, preferred stock owners are usually taken care of before common stock owners.

Once it decides which type of stock to issue, the underwriter determines what the best offering price should be. The underwriter is usually a large financial service company such as an investment banking firm or insurer whose sole responsibility is to raise as much money as it can for the company it is taking public. This is important for you to know if you are planning to buy shares in the IPO market.

The process usually starts with the underwriter determining how many shares will be issued. Once the price is determined, a date is set for the first day of trading for these shares. It can be difficult to get initial shares in a company that's going public because many brokerage firms that work with the underwriters offer IPO shares only to their best customers, as a gesture of thanks for their business. Although this may sound like a reward, IPOs can be risky investments. For the individual investor, it's tough to predict what will happen to the price of the stock on its initial day of trading or shortly afterward because at that point there is little, if any, historical data with which to analyze the company. Most of the news about IPOs comes from analysts who work for the underwriting companies, and a lot of that news is hype. Remember that the underwriter's responsibility is to raise as much money as it can for the company issuing the stock. The more hype the underwriter puts out, the more excited the buyers will be. The more excited the buyers are, the more they will pay per share for the stock.

Once the shares are issued, the risk shifts from the underwriter to the purchaser of the shares, and the IPO is complete. After investors have taken on the risk of owning these new shares, they have a responsibility to themselves to manage that risk because not all initial public offerings work out to be good investments. So if you choose this investment, make sure that you do your homework to find out whether the company has sound fundamentals and is participating in a market that is in strong demand.

Dividends

We introduced the concept of dividends in the previous discussion of common and preferred stock. Over the years, many investors have been drawn to companies that offer quarterly cash dividends as a way to establish a steady income. A cash dividend normally comes out of the corporation's earnings or accumulated profits and is paid directly to shareholders. Dividends are declared by the company's board of directors and are taxable as income to those who receive them. The annual percentage of the dividend is usually termed the *yield*.

Let's say you invest in a company and pay $10 per share because you are attracted to a dividend that has a 4 percent yield. This means that at the end of the year you will wind up with $.40 as a cash payout for every share you own. Most companies pay this out on a quarterly basis, which means you will receive $.10 every quarter. Although this might not seem like much at first, long-term investors who get started early can reinvest their cash dividends into the stock to maximize their gains. In other words, you can ask your broker to set up your account so that the cash dividend is automatically invested back into your account to buy more shares of the same stock. Over time, the extra shares add up and generate their own dividends, which compound the returns to the account.

This is a strategy that works well in retirement accounts, such as individual retirement account (IRAs) in the United States or the registered retirement savings plan (RRSP) in Canada. Remember, the idea is to accumulate as many shares as you can over a long period of time. Your goal is to build a steady stream of cash payouts when it's time to retire.

Dollar Cost Averaging

If you make direct monthly contributions to your retirement or savings account, you should also consider dollar cost averaging, which is a technique used to offset fluctuations in market prices. It can also help to reduce the risk associated with making a single large stock purchase.

The strategy is fairly simple. Invest a fixed dollar amount each month in a particular investment, regardless of the share price. The most important thing to remember is that you don't invest in stocks or funds that are in a steady decline. Focus on stocks within a price range or stocks that are in steady upward trends. Realize that you should use the dollar cost averaging strategy only with companies that have a history of strong growth with consistent earnings. Investing in companies that have weak balance sheets or do not show strong growth is speculating.

Here's why dollar cost averaging can work for you. You invest a fixed amount of money each month and buy as many shares as your investment allows. Should the stock drop to a lower price, you can accumulate more shares at the lower price. If the stock goes up in price, you would buy fewer shares. The strategy is to take advantage of the price fluctuations while smoothing out some of the volatility in your account.

You can combine dollar cost averaging with dividend reinvestment. The dividends paid can be applied toward buying more shares, which will result in a faster accumulation of shares over time. Keep in mind that this is a long-term investment strategy that should be applied to stocks that have a history of upward to sideways price movement. It serves no purpose to apply dollar cost averaging to stocks that are heading to a price level of zero.

Mutual Funds

A mutual fund is a company that brings together money from many individual investors and then invests those funds in stocks, bonds, or other assets. In other words, a mutual fund is like a basket of investments, and you, the investor, can purchase a piece of that basket. You don't actually own any of the assets in the mutual fund, but you participate in the overall value of the basket. As the collective value of the basket's assets rises, you make money. If the assets in the basket lose value, you suffer a loss from the mutual fund.

Mutual funds are professionally managed by fund managers. Fund managers move money from one investment to another, creating an opportunity for you to diversify your investments by spreading the risk throughout the basket of investments. The investment decisions are left up to the professional money manager, so you don't have to constantly watch over your money. With that said, you should know that mutual funds carry the risk of loss. Although the fund manager's responsibility is to make profits for the people who invest money with them, you are the one who makes the decision to either enter or exit the fund. This means that you have full control over whether you want to risk your money in this type of market. As with stocks, you should make sure your mutual funds continue to trend upward; it is wise to check on the performance of your funds at least once a quarter.

Total assets held in mutual funds today are in the many trillions of dollars. Using dollar cost averaging rather than a lump-sum deposit is one of the best ways to invest in mutual funds. As a long-term investor with a goal of building your retirement dollars, you have more than nine thousand mutual funds to pick from, so your toughest job is making sure you pick the right funds!

There are many research tools and services to help you investigate and understand any mutual fund that you may be considering. One of the more popular services is Morningstar (morningstar.com), which offers a variety of tools for researching and rating mutual fund companies. Most of Morningstar's research tools are easy to use and free as well. Another good rating service is Forbes.com, which not only reviews funds and evaluates performance, but also grades the funds according to how well they perform in bull (up) markets versus bear (down) markets. Mutual funds are not inherently safe or superior investments just because they offer built-in diversification. Take the time to select the right mutual fund in the same way you select stocks or other investments.

Exchange-Traded Funds (ETFs)

Exchange-traded funds are similar to mutual funds in that they allow you to diversify your investment dollars within a basket of stocks. The main difference between mutual funds and exchange-traded funds is that ETFs trade on exchanges just like stocks. You can buy and sell them anytime while the markets are open. Mutual funds, however, are traded at the end of the day, after their *net asset values* (NAVs) are calculated. The NAV is simply the formal term for the total value of the basket. If you place an order to buy a mutual fund in the morning, your order won't be completed until after the trading day ends.

One of the most commonly traded ETFs is the Diamond Trust Series, which trades under the ticker symbol DIA. The "Diamonds," as they're known, trade like a stock and represent roughly $\frac{1}{100}$ of the value of the Dow Jones Industrial Average (DJIA). The DJIA is an index that tracks the top thirty stocks that are believed to present the strongest representation of the U.S. economy.

Back in the early 1900s, Charles Dow came up with the idea that there were certain companies that basically drove the U.S. economy, and over time it was shown that his ideas had some merit.

His famous Dow Jones Industrial Average became a big part of his research about market movements, which later became the basis for a series of principles he developed for analyzing market behavior, known as the Dow Theory. Although the Dow 30 is a small sliver of the overall market, it is watched more closely than any other index in the world. Charles Dow also founded *The Wall Street Journal,* which became one of the most respected financial publications in the world. An interesting fact about Charles Dow is that he never finished high school. Born in Sterling, Connecticut, Dow believed that business information was not the private province of brokers and tycoons. In writing about high finance, he used homely analogy and the language of everyday life.

ETFs became available in 1993 as a cross between stocks and mutual funds. Not only did they help investors improve their portfolio efficiency, they also lowered investment costs as compared to mutual funds, which had higher fees. Since mutual funds are actively managed by a team of investment managers, there is a relatively high cost to own them—often around one to three cents per year for every dollar invested. ETFs are benchmarked to an index, industry, or sector, so the cost to maintain the proper benchmark balancing is much lower. A typical ETF expense might be only one-tenth to one-half cent for every dollar invested.

ETFs also provide a benefit when compared against individual stock purchases. Understand that if you wanted to buy twenty stocks in an effort to spread your risk by not putting all your eggs in one basket, you would have to pay a separate commission for every stock you bought in your account. These commissions would mount up quickly, resulting in a lower return on your investment. When you buy an ETF you pay only one commission for a similar group of stocks, thereby lowering your overall transaction costs.

ETFs quickly grew in popularity as investors around the world jumped on board. Almost immediately, investment banks and brokerage firms introduced their own branded ETFs. Merrill Lynch came out with Holders, Barclays issued iShares, and Vanguard added

Vipers. The names of these ETFs depend on who created them, but the idea is the same: Give investors a choice through diversification.

There seems to be no end to the number of ETFs that can be developed, because the possible combinations of stocks are endless. You can have baskets of energy companies, pharmaceutical companies, food companies, and financial companies. The most important thing you should know is that you have choices. In fact, you have so many choices that it could make your head spin! So how do you choose an ETF? The same way you choose stock and mutal funds. Use this checklist to find ETFs that are right for you.

- Start with the major indices. You can buy ETFs for all of the major stock indices including the Dow Jones Industrial Average and the S&P 500.
- Decide which industries or sectors you want to add to your investments. An advisor may help you with this choice. Select an ETF that follows the industry you choose.
- Compare ETF expense ratios. If two ETFs track the same industry but one costs 0.12 percent and the other costs 0.48 percent, save money with the lower-cost ETF.
- Research your ETF at any popular online financial site, such as Yahoo! Finance or your broker's site. You can see the top ten stocks in the ETF, historical performance, and much more.
- Even though ETFs have built-in diversification, don't put all of your money into one ETF. You still need to spread your risk around.

● CHATTER BOX AJ

I have a close friend who worked hard for twenty-five years for a company she believed in. Each month she contributed to her retirement account, and each month she bought stock in her company, with a plan to live out her golden years in comfort and style. Year after year this company continued to profit, and for more than two decades she watched her account grow in value. Her account balance had grown to more than $2 million, which was more than she ever had hoped for—but she deserved it. She dedicated her professional life to this company, and, like other employees, she helped build what was one of the most successful companies in the corporate world.

Then, in the late 1990s, three years before the day she was going to retire, it happened: Lucent Technologies' stock plummeted, losing 99 percent of its share value in a relatively short time. The real tragedy in this story is that the employees never saw it coming, nor did they have enough time to react to the news. Employees across the board watched helplessly as their retirement accounts vanished before their eyes. This is just one of the many stories I could tell about people who overlooked the importance of spreading risk through diversification. Please don't let this happen to you. Be sure to diversify!

Real Estate, Bonds, and Gold (Oh My!)

Diversification is a risk management strategy that mixes a variety of investments in a portfolio instead of concentrating the funds in any one investment. A good analogy for the way diversification works is to think of yourself as a businessperson who owns a sporting goods company. You could do very well selling golf clubs as your only product, but what happens during the winter season? Diversification means investing in an additional product that hedges your risk during the winter months. Adding snow skis to your product line would be a perfect way to diversify. If you want to diversify even more, you might add rain gear for outdoorsmen during the rainy months and sunglasses for the summer months. It is much wiser to spread out your investment dollars out so you can make sales during any season. So in addition to diversifying your investments in the stock market, explore how you can spread risk through different types of investments.

Real estate is an investment that most people are familiar with, especially those who own a home. Owning your home is a great way to build equity and net worth, but there are many types of real estate investments to consider. Many investors choose to use self-directed IRA funds to pay for rental properties, foreclosure properties, business franchises, and more. Before you put money into real estate, however, you should consult with your tax advisor or other financial professional to make sure you understand the restrictions that apply to this particular type of investment.

Bonds are a smart way to diversify your investments as you get closer to your retirement years. Investing in bonds is a relatively secure way to develop an income stream from your money. The issuer of the bond is essentially a borrower who receives money from you and promises to return the money with interest. You are the lender when you purchase a bond because your money becomes a loan of sorts. The term of the loan is outlined in the bond agreement, and an interest rate, called the *coupon,* is locked in at the time you buy the bond. The *maturity date* is the day on which the cash is given back to you—in other words, the end of the loan.

This chapter would not be complete if we didn't talk about one of the oldest investments in the world: gold. This precious metal has served humankind well for thousands of years. From the ancient Egyptians to modern-day investors, gold has been the universal currency and the best form of money civilization has ever known. It is the preferred investment of many, especially during times of economic or political uncertainty.

Purchasing gold is not as hard as you might think, but don't just jump at the first television commercial or Web advertisement without knowing a little about the fees and delivery charges. There are many places to purchase gold coins directly, where you actually take delivery of the physical gold. As you might have guessed, there are gold ETFs. These funds buy the gold for their basket, and then you purchase a share of that basket, as we discussed earlier. As with any other investment, start small and build your portfolio as you become more familiar with the market.

Limitless Possibilities

Be excited about the investment choices you have, along with the opportunities around you. You can get started with as little or as much money as you like, but the important thing is that you get started. Focusing on the possibilities helps you stay excited about the future. As you build your confidence in your own ability to profit from these investments, success will follow. The best is yet to come!

PART TWO

The Players

Chapter 4

Know Yourself

You can't take charge of your finances until you take charge of yourself. A disciplined investor is not born from an undisciplined personality. Cultivate your financial discipline with the eager anticipation of someone who expects it to grow and bear fruit!

Taking charge of your money is a business that requires time, patience, and energy. If this is more than just a hobby for you, then it makes a lot of sense if you treat your money the way all professionals treat their business plans. Let's face it, if creating a personal fortune was easy, everyone would be doing it. But don't confuse things that are easy with those that are simple. It's a lot easier to get yourself into financial trouble than it is to create financial independence. However, understand that the steps for creating financial independence are simple. You just have to get things moving in a positive direction.

Motivation!

In order to master the steps that allow you to take charge of your money, it is essential that you know exactly what motivates you. If there is one obstacle that prevents average people from realizing their own ability to achieve financial success it is their lack of motivation. Take a look at the people around you and notice the difference between those who are motivated in their work and those who are not.

We're sure you have seen individuals who are full of energy and excitement, with personalities that exude optimism and friendliness. Have you taken a hard look at these people to see what drives them to be this way? One of the main reasons for this type of behavior is that driven individuals most likely love what they are doing for a living. If they don't love their jobs, then they most certainly love their lives or at least their positions in life. In contrast to this, you've probably seen someone sitting at a desk in an office in that I-can't-wait-to-get-out-of-here trance. He stares at his watch, hating every minute of every hour of his working day. You don't have to ask him whether he enjoys his work, because it's written all over his face. It would be hard for you to miss the ever-present frown and lack of enthusiasm.

The sad thing is that a person like this could change his state of mind in an instant if he had the will and desire. Instead, he's made a decision to stick with the status quo and not make a change for the better, which, in turn, results in one of the great tragedies of existence: living in the doldrums of inactivity and stagnation. This is not a foundation on which a house of success is built, financial or otherwise.

Whether this applies to his job, relationships, or financial position, this person has made a decision to do nothing to improve his life. Most people in this position prefer to continue traveling along the status quo highway, hoping that one day things might get better, rather than taking responsibility for their own lives and forcing themselves to change.

People continue to endure this torture because over the years they have allowed themselves to be conditioned to think this way. Their parents might have taught them to believe that life offered little in the way of opportunities. Or maybe it was the way they were treated by an abusive spouse that made them think they didn't deserve to have pleasures in life. Perhaps the lackluster teaching style in school alienated them and left them pessimistic about the possibilities of future success. One of Albert Einstein's teachers reportedly told Einstein's father that regardless of what he did, Albert would never amount to anything. Imagine what the world would have missed if Einstein had taken this to heart and fulfilled that misguided prediction! Whatever the source, this negative conditioning results in what we call the "flea circus" mentality.

Are You Living in a Flea Circus?

Fleas can jump extremely high for their size, which is how they normally get from one animal to the next. If you were to catch a flea and put it in a jar without a lid, it would be easy for the flea to escape. In the old story of the flea circus, the trainer quickly put a lid on the jar after capturing these tiny creatures. Whenever the fleas tried to jump—*Bang!*—they would hit the lid and fall back down into the jar. Over and over, the fleas would try to jump, and every time they would fall back down. After a while the fleas got tired of hitting the lid; they would continue to jump just high enough to reach slightly below it without hitting it.

Seeing this for yourself you might think these fleas were pretty smart, but your opinion of them would change if you saw what happened when the lid was finally removed. The fleas would continue to jump to a height just below the lid, but they wouldn't jump any higher. They had been so conditioned that they simply gave up trying to explore the world beyond the jar. They stayed in place, refusing to try again, and eventually settled for life in the jar.

In a similar way, people who have given up on attaining the sweet things in life never venture beyond their five-foot by five-foot cubicles. They sit there all day long looking at their watches, bored and confused about where life is taking them. They have ceased to believe that they will ever achieve the goals they once had when they were young. The tragedy of negative conditioning is real and has direct consequences for individuals and families.

What would happen to the fleas in the jar if, with just one more attempt, they were able to jump over the edge of the jar and free themselves? What would change in the lives of those who made one more attempt to move beyond their corporate cages? It doesn't matter where you are in your life. Once you decide to get a taste of that freedom, the possibilities are endless.

Remember those motivated people we mentioned who love their jobs? This group includes the person working at the airport ticket counter with a big smile on her face as she helps a distressed passenger who has lost his baggage. It includes the cheerful restaurant waiter who is sincere when he asks if you are enjoying your meal. It includes the grocery store clerk who is happy to help you carry your bags out to the car, not because someone told him to, but because this teenager is excited about where he is in life and has not yet lost sight of the possibilities that await him.

Where are you right now? Have you lost sight of your goal? Or are you totally focused on the plan you have created for yourself, knowing that there is no limit to the things you can achieve? Go ahead and jump one more time!

● **CHATTER BOX AJ**

As we travel from place to place, through airports, hotels, restaurants, and grocery stores, we run into people like those we have described. What a pleasure it is to meet them! They are refreshing, and their attitudes are contagious. This is the approach you need to take if you want to create true wealth for yourself. Now is the time to make the decision to take action and follow through with your own plan. Don't waste a single minute. Just do it.

Find Your Hot Buttons

If you are looking for an endless supply of energy to "keep on movin' on," then you need to find out what your hot buttons are. A hot button is a trigger that helps motivate you to achieve your goals. For some people, this hot button is triggered when they think about the car they have been eyeing at the dealership. The mere thought of getting behind the wheel invigorates them. Young married couples might find their hot button when they look at pictures of the dream house they plan to own one day. Parents may be motivated when they look at their young children, understanding that a good financial plan will help them provide for their family. Others find that they get a boost of energy when they are giving to those who are less fortunate.

The people who are most driven possess a certain quality that propels them toward a higher purpose. If you are lucky enough to discover one of your own triggers, then nothing will stop you; the rewards you receive will be far greater than if you were just looking out for yourself. The main point is that you discover in yourself that which motivates you the most. Once you have found out what your hot buttons are, write them down.

Pain and Pleasure: The Great Motivators

Without question, pain and pleasure are the greatest motivators of all. Responding to pain and pleasure is the way we learned as children, and it's what still drives us as adults. (We're reminded of the joke about cooking bacon in your underwear; try it, and you'll immediately gain an appreciation for the rapidity and efficiency of pain as a motivator.) It's really not hard to understand the degree to which pain motivates us to move in the opposite direction.

On the other hand, we are just as readily motivated to move toward the refrigerator when we think of that container of rich, creamy chocolate ice cream loaded with fudge brownie bits that resides there. The pleasure we anticipate from the sweet taste of the ice cream moves us toward the fridge, while the memory of the pain from the splattering hot bacon grease moves us away from the stove. Pain and pleasure cause us to move, or behave, in certain ways, but it's in combination that the two cause the most movement. The trick is learning how to control these two reactions so that they work *for* us and not *against* us.

Pushing Your Buttons

In order to tap into your internal energy source, you should follow this simple rule when working toward your goal:

> *Focus on the pleasures of accomplishing your goal, while at the same time imagining the pain you will suffer should you not accomplish that goal.*

Here is a simple example that applies this rule to a common goal that people have. Let's say that you want to get back in shape, and your goal is to lose ten pounds. Many people find this difficult because the pleasure of eating is far too great. Focusing on the pleasure causes them to break down and go off their diets. This example illustrates how the pleasure of eating can result in more harm than good. In this case, you, the dieter, must reverse the pain/pleasure equation so that the feelings work *for* you instead of against you. You do this by focusing on the pleasure of accomplishing your weight loss goal rather than focusing on the pleasure of eating the food you enjoy so much. Then you imagine the pain you will suffer should you not reach that goal.

Conditioning yourself to focus on how great you will feel being ten pounds lighter instead of focusing on how good the food tastes is one way to think of it. You can also focus on how good you will look in those new clothes and all the extra energy you will have once you've accomplished your goal. You need to simultaneously reinforce this for yourself by focusing on how painful it will be should you not reach your goal. You must imagine the lack of energy and the tiredness you will feel as a result of overindulging. Focus on the disappointment you will experience when you have to shop for clothes in a bigger size. You can generate even more pain by contemplating the possible physical side effects of being over-weight: diabetes, heart disease, stroke, and some types of cancer. When you have created sufficient pain, you will be more motivated than ever to resist the temptation of the ice cream and embrace the pleasures of eating healthier foods.

Pain and Pleasure for Profit

We can apply the same principles in the world of finance. Just re-place the fudge brownie ice cream with your credit card in the ex-ample. The next time you feel the urge to splurge during a shopping trip, stop and remember the pain/pleasure rule. Instead of focusing on how great it would be to have that new set of golf clubs, focus on the pain of having a larger credit card bill at the end of the month. Instead of zeroing in on the pleasure of getting that hole in one with your new driver, focus on the satisfaction you will experience by paying down some of your debt with the extra cash you just saved.

Of course, this takes a lot of discipline and conditioning, just as a diet and exercise program does. Over time, though, you will dis-cover that the pain/pleasure rule works if you apply it consistently. Start off with small steps, making minor adjustments to your spend-ing habits. Eventually you can take on bigger challenges as you strive to change your strategies for making money.

Picture This

So far in this chapter we have discussed the differences between motivated individuals and those who are not so inclined to make positive changes in their lives. We have talked about the flea circus mentality in people who have simply given up trying. We have ex-amined ways to identify hot buttons and use pain and pleasure to keep things moving in the right direction. Now we need to address the image you have of yourself.

The mental picture you have of yourself is crucial in developing your plan to take charge of your money now. Can you imagine yourself having great wealth and being happy with this picture? If so, then things will be a lot easier for you as you continue to work on your financial plan. We mention this because money has a certain way of magnifying one's personality. Many people come into money, yet they remain unhappy with their lives. Money doesn't change a person's self-esteem. If you have a low opinion of yourself now, chances are you will still have a low opinion of yourself after you have made your fortune—you'll be wealthy and insecure, rather than just insecure.

This is why we recommend that you work on your self-image as seriously as you work on your business plan. The journey you are about to take involves much more than just learning how to take control of your finances; it involves a plan for overall self-improvement and personal success. Unfortunately, conditioning is also the root cause of feelings of low self-worth.

Taking charge of your finances also means taking control of your thoughts. You must come to believe in yourself to the point where you feel almost invincible. Nothing is impossible if you put your mind to it. You've probably heard the saying "Aim for the moon because even if you miss you'll still be among the stars." Make it a point to surround yourself with people who are goal oriented, optimistic, healthy, and fun to be with. Select friends who are likable and keep their minds open to new ideas that stimulate the thought process. When you get together, arrange brainstorming sessions to propagate new moneymaking ideas. When your self-esteem is high, you conduct yourself differently. People notice this, and you become a magnet for business opportunities that you may not have thought possible.

This is not some kind of crazy magic or feel-good nonsense. It is a fact of life that a positive mind-set attracts positive people into your life, just as the opposite is true for people with negative personalities. Those who are constantly negative attract problems to

themselves and then spend their free time wondering why everything in their lives is so bad.

● CHATTER BOX **AJ**

Rick and I were working with a particular gentleman to help him develop his business plan. We were having tremendous success, and he
was moving rapidly toward his financial goals. The future looked
bright, and the plan was coming together nicely. However, we noticed
that our student had a tendency to ask questions in a negative fash-
ion, constantly looking for "what was not working." You're no doubt
familiar with the old metaphor of the glass being either half-full or
half-empty; well, this client always seemed to see the glass as half-
empty. We continued to work with him despite his negative outlook,
but both Rick and I came to the conclusion that regardless of the success of our plan for his financial success, this person had conditioned
himself to think negative, and it had become a way of life for him. He
made money with us, but we realized that as soon as we sent him off
on his own, things would start rolling backward.

The negative thinking didn't just get in the way of his learning
new ideas about creating wealth; it eventually destroyed a business
relationship with his wife that would have been quite profitable for
both of them. Negative thinking and low self-esteem are destroyers of
opportunity. Protect the mental picture you have of yourself and avoid
contaminating those around you with negative energy.

Paint a New Mental Picture

Prepare yourself: There will be times when the steps you take to
improve your financial and mental state will be uncomfortable.
Moving outside of your comfort zone forces you to explore new
ways to grow and succeed. Following is a list of some simple things
you can do to paint a new picture of the person you will become. At
first, some of these activities might seem almost ridiculous. Humor

us for twenty-one days, though, because twenty-one days makes a habit, and you will see a positive difference!

- When the alarm clock rings in the morning, launch yourself into a new day with new opportunities. Sit straight up in bed, clap your hands, and in a loud voice, say, *"Yes!"* (Of course, you might want to give your spouse advance notice of this change in your routine, or you will only do this once!) This immediately revs up your engines and gives you a head start on carrying through with your financial plan. Be excited when you do this, and try your best to look forward to the next morning, when you will do the same thing. Do this every morning.

- Force yourself to smile at times when you just don't feel like smiling. If you don't believe this works, then close your eyes and think about your mental state right now. While your eyes are closed, force a smile on your face and notice the positive change in the way you feel. The change will be slight, but it will be positive for certain.

- Throughout the day, write down positive things that happen to you—immediately after they have happened. Creating this diary forces you to look for the positive in your daily life rather than focusing on the negative. We encourage our own children to maintain a "thankful journal" in which they record the three events from their day for which they are most thankful.

- Try to take a walk at least three times a week, either in the morning or right after your evening meal. As you walk, focus on your accomplishments while zeroing in on your top priorities for the week. This maximizes your efficiency without wasting your time by having to think too long about what is on your to-do list. It also helps you muster the positive energy you need to carry you over any bumps along the way.

- Monitor your own speech. Listen to the words that you use and the thoughts that cross your mind. Every time you hear a negative statement, take note of it and do your best to reframe the statement in your mind so it is more positive. This action step is something you cannot ignore, although it may be the toughest one of all because we often don't realize how we have positioned ourselves. You might hear yourself talk, but chances are that you have not been measuring the balance between the positive and negative statements you make during the day. Taking this step will make the most difference, not only in your financial life, but in your personal life as well.

The actions we have just outlined may not feel comfortable when you are performing them during the first few days, but you will soon begin to see results. Most people around you will not even notice that you are going through these exercises. After several weeks people will notice a positive difference in you. When this happens, take note of it. Write it down in your Positive Actions diary. This diary is your evidence that your life is moving in a positive direction and you are well on your way to taking charge of your money and your life!

Great Expectations

Remember that positive people enjoy associating with other positive people. Most of these individuals go out of their way to avoid negative thinkers, so keep that in mind as you monitor your language. Staying positive attracts business opportunities to you, and those opportunities bring along additional sources of revenue. Don't wish for it; expect it!

Wherever you are in life, celebrate your new beginning. Look at each day as a fresh opportunity to go out and make a positive change in your life. At first the changes may seem subtle, but over time you will recognize an acceleration in your achievements. Once this happens, people around you will be asking for advice, because everyone is going to want what you have. Count on it.

Finally, we hope you will share these ideas with those who are closest to you. Do this after you have seen results in your own life. When you have witnessed these changes on your own, you will be more convinced than ever that this is something you should give to those who need it. Let's face it, you can avoid negative thinkers at work and you can avoid those who want to contaminate you through the media and in public, but you can't avoid your family. Helping them ultimately helps you maintain a positive frame of mind, which in turn keeps you on track to carry out your plan and realize your ultimate dreams.

Chapter 5
Who's Watching Your Money?

Taking charge of your money requires that you take the charges away from your money. Fees and expenses are corrosives to your wealth; no one fee will hurt you, but the accumulated effects over time will topple your financial house as surely as a catastrophic storm.

Do you feel as though you're ill prepared to take charge of your money? Remember that one of the keys to success is not how much you know but how well you discipline yourself. Your biggest challenge is not your head but your heart. You should certainly continue your financial education throughout your life, but don't ever convince yourself that you're not smart enough to take charge of your own money.

Furthermore, you should know that nobody cares about your money more than you! There are many advisors, planners, banks, brokers, and managers who can provide important advice and services. Many of them are respectable and well qualified and will help you along your financial journey. But you should carefully weigh the pros and cons before you completely abrogate your financial responsibility and turn it over to a money manager. If you truly want to take charge of your money now, then you need to learn to use the resources available to you in the best way rather than finding a place to park your money and hoping for the best.

One of the key lessons we've learned in our years of working on and with Wall Street is that there is always going to be someone who wants to have a hand in managing your money. From the firm where you open your account to the broker who sells you the products to the software company that processes your trades, there is an opportunity on every corner to spend a little bit more than you should. The reason is simple: They charge a small fee for their part in the process, and the more money they have a hand in, the more profit goes to their pockets. Keep in mind that each fee is very small, so you don't really feel the pinch. Professional traders don't take these fees and charges lightly. They watch them like hawks and never pay a dime more than they have to. They know that they need to minimize the nuisance fees in order to take charge of their money.

In this chapter we want to equip and empower you to make the right decisions when it comes to selecting a company or individual to help you with your investing. You are the boss here! If a company or manager isn't doing the job you need them to do, then you get to say "You're fired!" Don't be intimidated by fancy language and well-appointed offices. It's your money, and you're the one who decides what's best for you and your family.

There are three major choices that you need to make to get started:

- What type of account(s) should I open?
- Which bank or broker should I do business with?
- Who should help me with advice?

We'll cover each decision in this chapter and give you ideas on how to get the most bang for your buck. Taking charge of your money is a combination of getting the most growth and paying the least in expenses. We'll also talk about some of the danger zones in this decision process so that you can steer clear of the mistakes before you make them.

Savings and Investing Accounts

Savings Accounts

The simplest type of account that many people start with is the tried-and-true savings account. The actual details pertaining to savings accounts can vary from one institution to another, but the basic concept remains the same. These accounts are designed to encourage savings; thus, they discourage withdrawals.

A typical savings account pays a nominal interest rate to entice you to keep your money sitting in the account. Some require a minimum balance, but most allow you to begin saving with whatever amount you have initially. That makes these accounts great for young savers. Getting your children into a basic saving program through a simple savings account is one of the best financial lessons you can teach. Every time they get a few dollars for a chore, encourage them to take a portion of their earnings to the bank to add to their savings accounts. Although the amount may seem trivial, the discipline that they're learning is every bit as important as the money that they're growing.

Since savings accounts are not intended to be high-transaction accounts, there is usually a higher cost associated with withdrawals, check requests, and other transactions. One of the reasons that financial institutions pay interest on these accounts is that they are able to keep the account maintenance costs low. It doesn't cost a bank very much to accept deposits into the account. However, it does start to cost them money when there is a lot of activity in the account. So keep that in mind when you open your savings account. It's called a savings account because it should be used for your savings.

Checking Accounts

A checking account is the account that is normally used for your day-to-day transactions. This account is intended for your check writing, bill paying, ATM withdrawals, and other transactions that you need for family operations. There are a lot of variations in the way checking accounts are structured, so you should carefully determine your needs to make sure that you're not getting too many features or too few features with your checking account. If you choose too many, you'll end up losing out on potential earnings or your basic fees will be too high. For example, let's say you write about ten checks per month. If you choose a checking account that gives you fifty free checks per month, you're receiving too much benefit that you're not using. A checking account that gives you fifty free checks per month might pay interest only if your account balance is above $10,000. On the other hand, you might find a checking account that allows twenty free checks per month and pays interest if your account balance is above $2,500. As you can see, the latter account meets your needs and pays interest much more quickly than the former account.

One of the enticements offered with many checking accounts is ATM fee rebates. With ATM fees in the range of several dollars per transaction, these fees can really add up. Don't look at these fees as a cost of doing business. Even though $3 is only 3 percent of a $100 withdrawal, that takes a big bite out of your account! If you could add 3 percent to your account, the increase in the growth of your money would be significant over time.

Consider all the possible fees when you're choosing a checking account. Besides the ATM fees, there are check fees, live teller fees, overdraft fees, and many more. We'll discuss these in more detail a little later in this chapter. For now, you need to determine which fees you might be subject to and then choose the account that keeps those to a minimum.

Brokerage Accounts

The brokerage account is a step up from the savings and checking accounts, although it may serve both of those purposes equally well. In fact, many brokerages have added the checking and transaction features to their accounts in order to provide a one-stop account. The main feature that distinguishes a brokerage account from a traditional savings or checking account is the ability to buy and sell securities with ease. That's right—this is the account for trading and investing.

A brokerage account can be set up as a cash or a margin account. A *cash account* simply means that any mutual funds, stocks, or other investments that you buy must be paid for in full with cash deposited into the account. A *margin account* allows you to borrow a portion of the purchase price of the stocks or funds. It is, quite simply, a loan from your broker, and the stock you purchase is the collateral. For example, if you want to buy $25,000 of ABC mutual funds and you have only $20,000 cash in your account, you can borrow the $5,000 balance if you have a margin account. Of course, as with any other loan, you will be required to pay interest on any amount that you borrow. Keep in mind that brokerage accounts don't have the margin feature added automatically. You have to complete a separate margin application, and the feature is added after your application is approved.

Retirement Accounts

Saving for retirement has tax advantages if you use a retirement account. There are some variations among retirement accounts, and their structure is subject to change at any time by changes to the tax laws. As a rule, retirement accounts allow you to save and grow your money without having to pay income or capital gains taxes on either the deposits or the earnings. The result is that the money in the account grows at a faster pace than with a standard brokerage account since the value isn't reduced each year by the amount of the taxes paid.

The traditional individual retirement account (IRA) allows you to deduct the amount of your annual contribution from your taxes. This means that the money you deposit into your account each year is tax free. Of course, there is a limit to how much you can deposit and get the tax benefit. The value of your account grows without being taxed; the taxes are paid when you reach retirement age, and then any withdrawals are taxed at whatever income tax bracket rate you fall into at retirement.

The Roth IRA is a newer type of account that allows you to make deposits with money that has already been taxed. This is referred to as *after-tax* dollars. As with the traditional IRA, Roth IRA accounts then grow tax free year after year. The benefit of the Roth IRA is that when you reach retirement age, all withdrawals are tax free.

Let's assume you have $1,000 to invest in an IRA and you're in the 20 percent tax bracket. If you place the entire $1,000 in a traditional IRA, you don't have to pay any taxes now. If your account is worth $5,000 at retirement, the entire $5,000 will be taxed at your current tax rate when you retire. On the other hand, you could pay the $200 tax now and deposit the $800 balance into a Roth IRA. When you retire, the Roth IRA may be worth $4,000, but the entire $4,000 may be taken out tax free.

Accounts for Kids

Accounts that you can set up for your children or grandchildren generally fall into two main categories: custodial accounts and education accounts. Since children can't legally manage their own finances directly, these accounts are set up for the benefit of the children but are managed by an adult until the children reach the legal age at which they can begin to take charge of their own money.

A *custodial account* can usually be opened with a very small initial deposit—sometimes as low as $100. For that reason, this can be a great choice for someone who wants to make a gift to a child for a birthday or other special occasion. There are often tax advantages for both the individual giving the money and the child, since tax rates on custodial accounts are lower than those on standard brokerage accounts. Once a custodial account is opened, you can continue to make contributions to it. So if you choose to open an account with a $100 birthday gift, you can deposit $100 as a birthday gift each year thereafter.

The money in a custodial account is owned by the minor child and will be in the child's control when he or she reaches the legal age (which varies from state to state). However, the good news is that you can use the money for the child's benefit, such as for education. Don't lose sight of the fact that your goal here is to save money for your child, not create a pool of free cash to tap into whenever you want. Discipline is the key to taking charge of money—whether it's for you or for your children.

An *education savings account* is a little bit like an IRA except that your savings goal is college, not retirement. As with the IRA, there are limits on how much you can deposit into an education account. But you also get tax breaks on the earnings in the account as long as the money is used for education expenses such as tuition, books, and room and board.

Keep It Super Simple

One of the dangers that many people fall into is failing to keep their accounts simple and in order. You don't necessarily need one of every type of account, and you don't need a different account for every type of investment. It's perfectly acceptable to mix stocks, bonds, and mutual funds in the same account.

● CHATTER BOX **Rick**

A couple approached me for advice regarding their retirement accounts. The first step is always to review the current situation to determine how to proceed. When this couple laid their account statements on the table, I was struck by the sheer volume of papers. I quickly realized that this couple was collecting accounts like some kids collect stamps. They seemed to have an account for every occasion. When I asked them why they had so many open accounts, they looked at me as though I didn't understand the basics of retirement planning.

Chatterbox continues

"Don't you think it's important to make a retirement contribution every year?" they asked.

I assured them that I certainly agreed that making an annual contribution was a good idea, but that still didn't explain why they had more accounts than some small-town banks. It turns out that this couple didn't realize they could make their annual IRA contribution to the same account each year. Instead, they opened a new account each time they wanted to make an IRA contribution. Needless to say, the first order of business was to consolidate all their IRAs into a single account.

Having too many accounts opens you up to several problems. First, it's very difficult to keep up with a lot of accounts. You should be reviewing your accounts on a regular basis to make sure that everything is in order. Look at balances, deposits, stocks you own, and so on. Whether you are at the point where you balance your accounts to the penny or simply look for major irregularities, you should never file the account statement without opening the envelope.

Second, every open account is an opportunity for thieves to steal your account information. We don't want you to be paranoid, but we do want you to be careful. It's a tragedy if you do everything you can to take charge of your money and then you lose control to a thief. Having a few key accounts is easier to manage and monitor.

Third, many accounts charge you basic account maintenance fees if the balance is below a certain threshold. When you consolidate your accounts, you can increase the balance in the remaining accounts and often have the various fees waived.

Finally, the fewer, the better when it's tax time. Each account that you have open will generate a tax report at the end of the year. How much easier is it to have only a handful of tax reports to sort through? If an accountant or tax professional files your tax forms for you, you'll likely pay a lower tax preparation fee if you don't inundate the person with account reports. At the very least, he or she should send you a thank-you card!

Going for Broke(er)

Figuring out where to keep your money is a crucial decision and can mean the difference between taking charge of your money or not. The endless choices of whom to do business with may seem overwhelming, but the decision is not as difficult as it may appear on the surface. In order to make the right choice, you simply need a good checklist of the basics. Once you've determined your own personal needs, it becomes a matter of picking the company that best serves those needs. We'll give you a manageable starter list to use, but feel free to add your own criteria as you see fit.

Location, Location, Location

With financial institutions, many people rate the old real estate adage as an important priority. As a rule, local banks have more local offices than larger banks or brokerages. Every rule has exceptions, and the trend with some of the larger firms is toward more local offices. This is also true with brokerage firms that have traditionally concentrated their business online. There is a growing recognition that people like to be able to walk into a local office and talk to a real person. In turbulent times, it helps to know that you are more than just a voice on the phone or an e-mail online.

Although you can conduct all your financial business remotely today, there can be an advantage to having a local broker or banker who knows you by name. There are occasions when you may need a loan, have a check to cash, or want to open a new account. It makes life a lot easier to sit down at a desk with someone who can walk you through the process. The person will be able to help you make decisions about the features you need so that you don't get too many or too few, as we discussed earlier in this chapter. This is especially true if you are fairly new to this business. The world of finances encompasses many choices, terms, and options, and it's good to know that you have someone close by to help you navigate.

Bigger Is (Not Always) Better

In recent years we have seen the downfall of some of the biggest names in the financial business. Lehman Brothers, Bear Stearns, and others came crashing down with dizzying speed. Many banks that survived were gobbled up by other banks. It got to the point where you walked into your local branch on Monday only to see that the sign over the door was different from the sign that had been hanging there on Friday. It used to be a rule that bigger is better; if you did business with a megafirm, you could rest confident that your money was in good hands. Clearly, that's not necessarily the case anymore.

However, there is no intrinsic safety in going with the small bank on the block. Indeed, in 2008, the Federal Deposit Insurance Corporation (FDIC) listed twenty-five bank failures for the year. Most of these banks were small local or regional banks that had come and gone without drawing the attention of too many people— that is, unless, you had accounts at one of those failed banks. Then the failure became very personal as you waited in an endless line outside a closed office for some word on the status of your money. You saved diligently, eliminated your debt, and took charge of your money. The only problem was that you couldn't get to your money because your bank had been shuttered. That's why choosing a bank or broker is such an important decision.

The fact is that there are many very strong small banks and large brokers. Size alone is not an adequate indicator of how safe your money will be. Unfortunately, history is no longer a good barometer either. Bear Stearns was founded in 1923 and was considered a fixture on Wall Street. So much for fixtures. Here are a few ideas to help you choose a safe haven for your accounts:

1. RATINGS

Let's face it—most of us have neither the time nor the expertise to digest a stack of financial reports from a bank or broker that we're considering. Fortunately, there are services that will do that for us. A quick search online yields many different bank rating companies. These companies sort through the reports and data and generate a rating for each bank. The rating reflects the overall financial health of the bank based on the criteria they review. When you look at several different rating services, you can get a pretty good idea of whether or not your bank is on the tightrope. Several good services that you can explore are Bankrate.com, Fitchratings.com, and Veribanc.com.

2. INSURANCE

Almost all banks have the basic insurance coverage and then some. It starts with the FDIC, which protects your deposits up to $100,000. When the financial turmoil of 2008 started, the FDIC insurance was raised to cover deposits up to $250,000. It will likely change again to meet the needs of the marketplace. Next in line is the Securities Investor Protection Corporation (SIPC), which is held by most brokers. The SIPC protects you if you have stocks and cash with a broker who fails. When the troubled broker closes shop, the SIPC steps in and helps you recover your investments. Note that the SIPC protects you against your broker failing, not against falling stock prices! This insurance provides protection for up to $500,000. Beyond the FDIC and SIPC, many firms offer additional private insurance protection, often covering deposits up to many millions.

3. GROWTH

Whether a company is growing or not is a somewhat softer measure of its safety and strength, but it can be useful nevertheless. If a company is experiencing a financial crunch, the tendency is to pull in the reins and start cutting back on services and projects. You have to be careful with what you look at here. It can be a healthy sign for a company to consolidate a little and focus on its core business, so we're not talking about looking for banks that are spending like freewheelers. But find out whether the bank is getting new customers, maintaining its level of customer service, and continuing to offer solid products. Don't expect it to open a branch on every corner, but if it plans to open a few offices in strategic locations, that can be a sign of smart, disciplined expansion.

Online Access

If you haven't yet accepted the fact that we live in a wired world, now is the time to take that bold step. If you are really going to take charge of your money, you need to be able to put the tools and resources that are available online to work for you. It's really not a question of whether banks or brokers have online access but rather what tools they offer and how easy they are to use.

You would do well to get the best combination of high-tech, high-touch here. This concept was introduced by John Naisbitt in his 1982 bestseller, *Megatrends*. The premise is that the more we move toward technology, the more we need the human touch. So why not look for a company that gives you great online tools and access while still providing a friendly individual who can walk you through the details when you need help? Whether you walk into a local office or pick up the phone and talk to a friendly operator, find the company that lets you feel comfortable with your decision. Hey, if you can't get their attention and service when you're choosing a bank or broker, how well do you think they'll serve you after they have your money?

Software

Software is a different consideration from online tools and access because it is specific to your trading and investing. First you need to decide what you'll be doing with the software. Are you a trader or an investor? Most people are investors and will use the software only for buying some shares of a mutual fund or adding another certificate of deposit (CD) to their account. Most firms charge a lower commission for buying and selling stocks and bonds online rather than placing the order through a representative. Unless you just don't want the responsibility of buying and selling on your own, you need to be sure that the company you do business with has an easy-to-use software option that lets you place your own orders.

Don't hesitate to ask your banker or broker to walk you through your first couple of orders. Remember, they work for you! If they don't take the time to ensure that you know exactly how to place an order online, pack up your accounts and find someone who will.

Records and Reports

If you're meticulous in your record keeping and you know exactly where to find all of your account statements, tax reports, and deposit slips, congratulations! This section is for the rest of us mere mortals who find ourselves at the end of the month, quarter, or year lacking some vital information for filing taxes or reconciling statements.

Part and parcel with taking charge of your money is making sure you know what's going on. Have you ever written checks on your account and received an overdraft notice because that deposit you thought you had made last week was still sitting on your desk at home? Then you're one of the many who should harness the power of online reports to keep track of your money. Wall Street professionals never guess about what they've bought or sold, how much they paid, or whom they traded with. You'll never find professional traders who can't give you any details you want about their transactions. Manage your money with the same attention to detail and record keeping.

The basic reports are the handiest. Look for a company that lets you view your monthly account statements. Along with that, it's very helpful to be able to search for transactions by date and type. Not sure whether you made that deposit last week? No problem! Just sign in to your account and search for "deposits" in the last thirty days. You'll see a list of all the deposits made to that account, and you'll immediately know whether you have money to cover the checks or whether you need to run to your desk and grab the abandoned deposit.

At the end of the year, both you and your accountant will be thankful if you're doing business with a bank that lets you download your transactions for the year into a simple spreadsheet file. If you need it in a nice, compact format, then you can download your compiled tax report, which includes gains and losses, dividends, and other key information that the IRS can't live without.

Fees

You'll notice that no broker or bank will ever send you a bill at the end of the year for several thousand dollars for charges like ATM withdrawals, check fees, or annual account fees. When the fees are charged a few dollars at a time and spread out over the year, they seem a lot less painful. And when the fees don't hurt or catch your attention, you're more inclined to pay them without protest. It's one of the reasons that income taxes are deducted from your paycheck. Our elected officials know that they'd have a revolt on their hands if you had to write a check at the end of the year for the total amount of your taxes. If the fees, charges, and expenses can be kept small and buried in the details, you'll just keep marching in the parade. But if you are going to take control of your money, you need to minimize charges against it!

First of all, your objective is to balance fees with earnings. The account that has absolutely no fees may not be the best choice if the bank doesn't pay you any interest on your account balance. In other words, if you have a choice between an account with no fees or interest and an account that charges you $100 in fees but pays you $200 interest, the latter is obviously the better choice.

Next, you need to break down the fees and charges and decide which account keeps these to a minimum. To help you make your decision, the following is a list of common fees that you should consider in your decision:

- Trade commissions
- Annual account fees
- ATM fees
- Check-writing fees
- Fees for using a personal teller versus online access
- Overdraft fees
- Minimum balance charges
- Account records and reports fees
- Bill pay fees
- Account transfer or closing fee
- Stop payment or returned deposit fee

As you can see, the list of possible fees is long and tricky. Make sure you take the time to read the fine print, and don't be afraid to ask your banker or broker about specific what-if scenarios that you think you might encounter. Even after you've opened your account, review it regularly to make sure that you still have the best account for your needs. Banks are constantly marketing new and varied account features, and they may have a better choice for you that wasn't available when you first opened your account.

Products and Research

When it comes time to buy or sell an investment, you need to be able to find the right product. That means that it has to be available through your bank or broker, and you need to be able to do a little research on the product. Many investors have a couple of basic index funds—mutual funds that simply follow one of the major stock indices such as the Dow Jones Industrial Average. This is a good way to start investing in the stock market without having to research individual companies. It's important that you choose an index fund with a low expense. There's no need to pay a lot to the fund manager of an index fund. Your bank or broker should provide research tools that let you find this kind of basic information quickly and easily.

Also, the company you do business with should have a good selection of products from which to choose. This should include stocks, mutual funds, bonds, and CDs. You need to be able to compare ratings and yields if you're looking for bonds. If you want to buy a CD, your aim should be good rates and maturities. With stocks, you'll want to know the basic company information and be able to dig deeper into the reports when you learn how to read through them. You probably won't use all of the research tools and reports that are available, but make sure that you will have access to the information you need. If you can't find what you want with your current broker or banker, ask. If you don't get the answer you want, use this chapter to help you find someone who will serve you better.

Security

The responsibility for security falls on both you and your broker or banker. You should take the proper precautions to make sure that your personal information doesn't fall into the wrong hands. Some simple steps include changing your account passwords often. You might have heard that passwords should be treated like toothbrushes— never share with anyone and get a new one regularly. Also, it's a great idea to have a paper shredder at home. That's a very good investment in your personal information security. When you're done with account statements, deposit receipts, or confirmation letters, turn them into confetti, unless you need to keep them in your records files.

Beyond the steps that you take toward information security, make sure your bank or broker does its part. Some firms that do a lot of business online offer secure cards that generate a password number. When you log in to your account online, you enter the password number rather than a password that you create. This number changes every minute or so, making it almost impossible for someone to steal your account password.

Make the effort to ask your bank or broker how it handles your personal security. What happens if your account information is stolen? What charges will you be responsible for if someone writes an unauthorized check? How does the bank or broker monitor your account activity to flag a possible breach in your account security? While you hope that you never fall victim to identity theft, the unfortunate reality is that many people will have to deal with it at some point. If that happens, you should make sure your bank or broker works for and with you, not against you.

Don't Keep Your Nest Eggs in One Basket Case

In spite of your best efforts to thoroughly vet your bank or broker, you may end up picking a company that you shouldn't be doing business with. If it's simply a matter of poor service, you can always fire the firm and find one that cares about your business. But there may come a time when you discover that the company you thought was solid is really just a house of cards. The old rule of thumb that you learned from your grandmother applies here: Don't keep all your money in one place. Make sure you have accounts with at least two firms. You can go too far with this idea and open accounts at every bank and brokerage you pass on the street. That's as bad as keeping your money in one place—even if that's under your mattress. If you spread your accounts among two or three firms, then you still have access to some of your money if one of those firms should experience trouble or even if it closes.

Picking Your Advisor

One day a financial advisor invited a prospective client to take a short trip with him. They hopped into the advisor's luxury sedan and crossed town to an exclusive neighborhood. After they entered the gated community, the advisor started pointing out various luxuries and amenities they saw as they passed.

"Look at that fine car in the driveway."

"Notice the beautiful stonework on that home."

"That is some of the best landscaping in town."

"See the wing on that home? That's an indoor swimming pool."

As they were wrapping up the tour and leaving the community, the advisor looked over at his prospective client and said, "Did you see all of those wonderful things as we drove through?"

"Of course, they were beautiful!" replied the client, with eager anticipation.

"Well, if you bring me all your business, buy the products I recommend to you, and let me make your financial decisions . . . one day all of that will be mine!"

Finding Diamonds in the Coal

The financial advisory business has many very capable, skilled advisors from which to choose. These people can be valuable additions to your list of resources to help you take charge of your money. But the industry is also rife with hucksters and unqualified advisors, who are hardly worth the label of "advisor" at all. In fact, their skills lie more in sales and relationships than in financial advising.

The bottom-line secret that most financial advisory companies don't want to admit to you is that the most money is made for them when you frequently buy high-margin products. There's just not a lot of profit motivation for the advisor if you stick your money in money market and index funds. With that in mind, you have to recognize that most of the people you talk to are sales professionals, not financial professionals. Oh, sure, they've passed the required tests and exams and have picked up enough lingo to impress you with their conversation. Don't be impressed with façades; make sure you carefully consider every recommendation before you commit your money.

● CHATTER BOX **Rick**

Early in my financial career, I briefly joined a firm that is known for its small, personal advisory offices. After going through the required firm training, I started my field training. As part of the field training, we were required to make a certain number of cold calls every day. During the course of the call, we were instructed to specifically ask for the sale from the client. The product that we were offering was the same for every client and it changed from week to week, depending on the sales focus of the firm. I was having trouble with the idea of trying to sell the same product to every client, so I requested a meeting with the regional manager.

We met for lunch one day, and I explained my dilemma. "You want me to try to get the client to buy a specific investment product, but what if that client doesn't need what we're selling?" I asked.

The regional manager reached for the salt shaker, pushed it across the lunch table, and positioned it directly in front of me. "If I tell you that we're selling salt shakers today, then every client you talk to will buy a salt shaker," he replied.

At that very moment I paused, pushed the salt shaker back across the table, and said, "If they don't need a salt shaker, they're not going to buy one from me." I excused myself from that lunch and promptly left the firm.

Unfortunately, this firm is not a glaring exception to the way many financial advisory companies do business. Take a closer look at how they recruit and train their "advisors," and you'll see the truth in advertising. First of all, the recruitment site draws in prospective advisors by asking if they want "more personal and professional freedom, greater financial rewards, and an opportunity to make a real difference." A real difference for whom? The financial rewards and real difference are clearly going to be for the advisor's benefit, not necessarily yours. Zoom in a little closer to the training plan and you'll see how much advice training your advisor is receiving. The advisor training program is almost ten weeks long and includes such key skills as:

- Prospecting
- Sales presentation skills
- Market research
- Developing referral sources
- Time management
- Calling prospects for orders and appointments

Your mental brakes should be screeching right about now. Do you see anything in there about understanding how markets work, learning how to manage risk for the client, or reading charts and research reports in order to conduct a proper technical and fundamental analysis of the investment they want to sell to you?

They may tell you that all advisors must pass the required regulatory exams before they can open for business. Here's another secret from Wall Street: Regulatory exams have almost no correlation to the skills of the advisor. First of all, in order to pass a regulatory exam that lets you sell investments, you need a score of only 70 to pass. Second, you have as many opportunities to take the exam as you need to pass it! Miss it once; take again it two, three, four times, or more. Finally, the preparation courses that many advisors take to get ready for the exam are designed for the sole purpose of getting a passing grade. Period.

The firm we just mentioned describes its training for exam preparation, telling you the "materials cover everything you need to know in order to pass the . . . exams." Notice that it doesn't say anything about advisor skills or proficiency. So when you walk into one of the firm's offices, you may very well be entrusting your money to someone who passed the exam by the skin of her teeth and yet has been thoroughly trained in the fine art of getting you to buy what she's selling.

Sales versus Advice

This leads us to the first rule for choosing an advisor who will work with you to help you take charge of your money. Look for an advisor who takes the time to ask questions and provide you with advice and guidance. Steer away from anyone who makes you feel like you're a prospect to sell to rather than a client to help. As we've described, many so-called financial advisors are really just smooth-talking salespeople who chose the financial business as a venue for plying their trade.

The following is a checklist of flags to help you sort the sales from the skills:

- *Find an advisor who asks questions first.* One of the key responsibilities of every financial advisor is determining client suitability. The advisor can do that only by asking first and selling later.

- *If the advisor aggressively pushes proprietary products, push back.* That doesn't mean that mutual funds and products offered by that firm are inherently bad. If they meet your needs, they may very well be good products. But understand that proprietary investments are usually the most profitable to the firm.

- *Check the credentials of your advisor.* As we've discussed, the regulatory licenses (Series 7, Series 66, etc.) are minimum requirements, not indications of expertise. The best advisors often have or are working toward some type of professional designation. The most common designations include the certified financial analyst (CFA), the certified financial planner (CFP), and the certified market technician (CMT). If your advisor doesn't have any professional designation, don't hesitate to come right out and ask what qualifies him or her to help you manage your money. It is far better for you to walk out on an offended advisor than to lose money with an unqualified advisor.

- *Is your advisor afraid of cash?* True financial advisors know that keeping cash in your account can be a sound part of your overall financial plan. Cash helps to reduce fluctuations in your account value and lets you take advantage of investment opportunities as they arise. A salesperson abhors cash like nature abhors a vacuum. If you have cash, the salesperson will not let you rest until you buy something.

- *A good investment advisor knows that your ability to take charge of your money means you have to consider all aspects of your finances.* The right advisor will take into consideration your debt, credit cards, outstanding loans, real estate, and other assets in order to determine which investments are right for you. Salespeople are interested only in the account that they can influence. They won't be interested in accounts that you have with other firms because they can't make any money on those. Besides, they'll reason, if you wanted their help with those accounts, you'd transfer the accounts to them.

Your Financial Fingerprint

No two people have the exact same financial advice needs. When selecting a financial advisor, look for someone who is willing to tailor a plan to your needs. Don't let someone squeeze you into a cookie-cutter plan that gets you out of the office in record time. There are a lot of financial portfolio review software packages that will crunch your investments and spit out a multicolored report, replete with charts and graphs, which looks like a Fortune 500 company annual report. A good advisor might use such a report as a starting point, not the end objective.

We mentioned the concept of suitability. There are some investments that may be perfect for one person and absolutely disastrous for another. You need to always be aware of whether or not your advisor is considering investments that are properly suited to your needs and objectives.

> ● CHATTER BOX **Rick**
>
> I recently heard a story about an elderly couple who got a call from their financial advisor. The crash of 2008 had taken a toll on their investments, and they lost almost half of their account value. The advisor told them that he had bad news: Based on the new value of their accounts, they had to reduce their living expenses by half.
>
> The first thought that crossed my mind when I heard this story is why in the world did that advisor have an elderly couple so exposed to the stock market that their ability to meet everyday expenses was put at risk? An elderly retired couple needs to have their investments protected. Growth and income are secondary to protection. A good advisor helps you understand these requirements, rather than passively sitting by while you take risks you shouldn't.

How Do You Manage Risk?

This question is not just for you; it is one you should ask your advisor. There are times when the best planning succumbs to a bad investment. Your stock starts to crash, bad news hits the market, or something else rocks your investments. You need to make sure that your advisor doesn't subscribe to the tenets of ostrich investing—just stick your head in the ground and wait until it all goes away. The problem with that approach is that your nest egg might all be gone when you pull your head back out!

There are a number of strategies that you and your advisor can use to manage risk. Here are some strategies to consider:

- Stock options to protect individual investments
- Market index options to protect your overall account

- Index and industry exchange-traded funds (ETFs), which provide diversification in a single investment
- Cash, which helps to smooth out the effects of rough markets
- Bonds and certificates of deposit (CDs), which provide stability and a little income
- Stop-loss orders, which will get you out of an investment if it turns sour

It has been said that poor investors watch their profits, while great investors watch their losses. Be a great investor and take charge of your money!

Indians or Chiefs?

When you're looking for a financial advisor, you need to know whether that advisor is actually making investment decisions or simply acting as the front person for placing your money with other advisors. It's not necessarily wrong if your advisor is parceling out your account to other advisors as long as he or she helps you maintain a close eye on what's happening with your money.

Take the case of Bernard Madoff, a former chairman of the Nasdaq stock market, who apparently swindled investors out of $50 billion through fraudulent investments and reporting. As news leaked out about the magnitude of the fraud, investors found that many advisors and mutual funds that they had been doing business with had, in turn, sent the money to Madoff to manage. One chief investment officer, who wasn't caught up in the downfall, said of those advisors, "It means that they didn't do their due diligence [as] they were supposed to and were chasing those returns."

When you're shopping for a financial advisor, use this list to help you determine the degree to which your advisor will be hands-on with your account:

- *Where will your funds be held?* This is called the *account custodian.* Make sure it's a solid, reputable firm.

- *Does your advisor use separately managed accounts?* These are accounts that are not managed by your financial advisor but by other advisors (known as subadvisors). They can offer you tax and investment allocation benefits that are better than those of standard mutal funds. Make sure you understand the process he or she uses to select these accounts. This process should be suited to your circumstances, not the advisor's commissions or cookie-cutter formats.

- *Does your advisor maintain diversification?* Having a friendly advisor who sends all your money to the same place is wrong. What happens if that basket falls with your eggs inside?

- *How often will your advisor meet with you to review the performance of your account?* Whether your advisor makes the investment decisions or not, he or she should review your account with you at least twice a year.

The Best Advice

As every Wall Street professional knows, getting good advice at the right time can be invaluable. The world of finances is complex and constantly changing. That makes it nearly impossible to be an expert in all the areas that you'll encounter as you make decisions to take charge of your money. The best advice you can take at this point is to carefully choose how, where, and with whom you do business. Keep it super simple (KISS), trust your judgment, and follow the guidelines we've provided.

Taking Charge Forward!
Savings and Investing Accounts

Okay, now you're ready for the action steps. Think of your accounts as the bricks you're going to use to build your financial house. You can build a house with the wrong bricks, but it will look funny and might fall in a storm. Take the time to open the proper types of accounts and the appropriate number of accounts. Don't worry about getting it exactly right the first time. This isn't a do-or-die proposition. If you make a mistake, you can always change it.

- Choose the proper account.
- Simplify your accounts—don't have too many.

Going for Broke(er)

Now get ready to pick the company that gets your business. All banks and brokers are not created equal. After a while they all start to look the same on the surface, but there are significant differences that lie deeper than the advertising slogans. You're going to be paying these people, so they work for you! If they ever quit working for you, fire them. You marry your spouse, not your banker. Stick with your financial company as long as it's helping you take charge of your money. When it starts trying to take charge of your money, bid the firm farewell and find a new one.

- Do business locally if you're new or inexperienced.
- Check the ratings, insurance, and growth of your bank or broker.
- Online access is a modern must.
- Do you have access to easy-to-use software?
- Records and reports on your investments make life a lot easier—especially at tax time.
- Minimize the fees you pay.
- Pick a company with a wide selection of products and research tools.
- Account security is crucial—you and your bank/broker should protect that.
- Diversify your accounts by having accounts with at least two banks or brokers.

Picking Your Advisor

Your financial advisor can be one of your greatest helpers or one of your greatest hindrances. Outside of your family and your spiritual leader, this person may be one of the most influential people in your life. Don't place your trust in just anyone. Take the time to interview the advisor and some of his or her other clients.

- Choose an advisor rather than a sales professional.
- Make sure your advisor is as concerned about making suitable investments for you as you are.
- Pick an advisor who is as hands-on as you need him or her to be.

Don't ignore your better judgment and assume that the advisor is smarter than you. If you're not getting the warm fuzzies, move on to the next prospective advisor. Common sense is unfortunately not at all common. Trust yours.

Chapter 6

If You're Not Angry, You're Not Paying Attention

Anger is emotional fuel. If you harness its power you can effect positive changes to take charge of your money. Anger alone, without change, will leave you and your finances in ashes.

You do realize that the biggest obstacle to taking charge of your money now is not your head but your heart, right? When it comes to money and finances, our emotions get in the way of what we often know is the right course of action. We recognize what we should do, but we don't do it. There are a number of reasons that this happens, but the bottom line is that money hits us in the heart and we do what feels good rather than what is best for us in the long run.

Do you hate debt more than you love material things? If you don't, then you need to start cultivating a healthy animosity toward debt. As you begin to do that, you'll quickly realize that you're surrounded by a multitude of enemies. We're not just talking about people who aren't being entirely helpful but also about those who are actively undermining your efforts to take charge of your money.

You might be thinking that what we've just said is pretty harsh. Yes, it is harsh language, but it's the ugly truth about modern consumerism. Entire industries thrive on the fact that most people won't be responsible with their money. They are the tigers in the forest, stalking unsuspecting travelers for their next meal. They are the wolves of predatory money tricks that are dressed in sheep's clothing. Their offers and enticements appear great on the surface, but they are rife with dangers and pitfalls. And if you venture into this territory without an understanding of where these dangers lie and who is peddling them, you will fall victim to them and lose control over your finances. However, if you recognize the source of the peril, you can defend against it and succeed in taking charge of your money.

One characteristic of professional traders and investors is that they are acutely aware of how they make money and how they lose money. They can tell you exactly what fees they're paying for their transactions, accounts, and other aspects of their business. You'll never hear professional traders lamenting the fact that they were manipulated into taking too much margin, paying transaction fees they weren't aware of, or buying stocks now and paying for them later. They count their costs, calculate the risks, and determine whether these risks and costs are worth the potential profit. Granted, they may make bad investment and trading decisions at times, but it is never due to the fact that they were lured by clever marketing or hidden agendas. They know the rules of the game, and they play with their eyes wide open.

If you want to really take charge of your money, you have to approach your finances with the same level of attention and wariness as a professional trader would. You need to start thinking, "No more Mister (or Ms.) Nice Guy." You are surrounded by a cacophony of marketing messages trying to entice you into spending money you may or may not have. The purveyors of these messages have no regard whatsoever for your financial well-being. For that reason, you need to approach them as you would approach an enemy—with a sharp eye and the determination to win.

In this chapter, we'll identify some of the most common traps that lie in wait for you. The four main topics discussed in this chapter—credit cards, cars, homes and real estate, and retail shopping—are the top financial obligations of most people; therefore, they contain the most danger spots. As you read through this chapter, take notes on areas where you think you are most susceptible. Then take the actions necessary to ensure that you never fall victim to these traps again.

Credit Cards

Zero Percent APR for the First Year

The APR is the *annual percentage rate,* or the amount of interest that you are being charged by the credit card company. Since credit cards are unsecured loans—that is, there is no collateral required to back up the credit line—they typically carry the highest interest rates. It is not unusual to see credit card interest rates of 20 to 30 percent or higher, even when the interest rate on savings is only 2 to 3 percent. Simply put, credit card interest expense is one of the greatest dangers to most family finances. The offer of a 0 percent APR for the first year is a marketing ploy to get you to move your balances from other credit cards to a new credit card. Worse yet, it can have the added effect of enticing you to spend more using the new card since you will have no interest expense for the first year. You start to think of the credit line as free money.

If you're well disciplined and you have a plan to eliminate your credit card debt, it might make sense to transfer your outstanding balances to a 0 percent APR card—assuming, of course, that you use the 0 percent APR grace period to actually reduce or eliminate your debt rather than increasing your debt or simply maintaining the status quo. However, as we'll discuss later in this chapter, by adding another credit account you could be reducing your credit score, which has a negative impact on your finances.

No Payments or Interest for Six Months

This has to be one of the most egregious marketing messages by any credit company. These types of offers are often made by retail store credit cards. The objective is twofold: first, to encourage you to make a purchase now rather than later and, second, to collect interest from you on the purchase. On the surface, it looks like they're being your best friend, offering you an interest-free, six-month loan. Some people will use this offer and pay the full balance without consequence, but many others enter into this agreement and lose. The key stipulation in this offer is that you must pay off the entire balance before the end of the six-month grace period. If you don't, you will pay interest retroactively to the original purchase date.

Let's say you get the invoice for your purchase and place it in your stack of bills to pay. Toward the end of the six months, you grab the invoice and write the check. You happen to miss dropping the check in the mail by a couple of days, and your payment arrives a day late. You are now responsible for the full six months of interest plus a penalty on the late payment.

This offer plays on the notion of "play now, pay later." You want a new dining room set but don't have the money? No problem! Need that big-screen TV before the big game? Go ahead! You've got six months to figure out the little details—such as where you will get the money. At the end of the six months, the novelty of the new purchase has worn off and you're saddled with a debt that may take months or years to pay off.

Credit Life Insurance

Insurance has a place in everyone's financial plan because it helps offset the risk of financial hardship in the event of a death or disability. Credit card life insurance generally provides for paying off the balance of the credit account. But credit card life insurance is sold to many people without any consideration given to suitability—in other words, is it something you really need?

Your first red flag should come from the way credit life insurance is sold. One of the tricks used by credit card companies is to send you a check. The fine print on the back of the check says that by cashing the check, you agree to the terms of the insurance policy. There you have it: You cash the check; they sell the policy. If it really is a good deal for you, why do they have to deceive you into purchasing it? Another approach is verbally offering the insurance for a free trial when you open your credit account. The salespeople often tell you that the call is being recorded so that they have the record of your verbal agreement. However, they don't spend a lot of time talking about the fact that your credit insurance covers only the card for which it is purchased. If you have five cards, you must purchase five credit insurance policies, one for each card. Also, rather than paying the balance, some policies pay only the monthly minimum for a specified period. They spend more time talking about how great the free trial is. And—oh, by the way—unless you cancel the coverage, you will be charged the insurance premium at the end of the free trial period.

As an alternative, you should review your primary life and disability insurance policies to see whether you have adequate coverage for all of your debts and obligations rather than buying insurance for your credit card accounts only. Too much insurance coverage can end up hurting your finances just as much as not having enough!

Too Many Credit Cards

Take a look through your wallet or purse. Between the major credit card accounts, gas cards, and retail store cards, how many different credit cards are you holding on to? There are several reasons to cut back on the number of cards you're carrying.

First, having too many open accounts negatively affects your credit score. Part of the calculation of your credit score is based on the total amount of your credit lines and how much of that credit is being used. Many people have open accounts that they aren't even aware of; they don't have the actual card and may not even have a balance on the account. But the fact that the account is still open affects your credit score and leaves you open to credit fraud.

Second, there is a real temptation to spend money if the account is open. Let's say you have a high balance on your major credit card account, so you're hesitant to spend on that card. So you open up a credit line with a store, and you get a $5,000 credit limit for that card. Now you begin to think that you have an extra $5,000 that you didn't have before. Open credit lines are an invitation to spend that nonexistent money!

Third, every account that you have open is a possible target for credit card fraud. Criminals are using increasingly sophisticated methods to steal your credit information. The more accounts you have open, the more targets there are for those criminals. You should be reconciling your credit card statements every month to watch for suspicious activity. The more cards you have to check, the harder it is to keep up with that task.

Penalties and Late Fees

Although the credit card companies say that penalties and fees for being late are to encourage you to be on time, the fact remains that this is a great revenue stream for them. If you send in a late payment, you are charged interest on the full balance as well as a hefty penalty. Along with that, many credit cards then increase your interest rate on the account. If you fall even further behind, you could find yourself exceeding your credit limit for that account and then having to pay additional penalties and a higher interest rate as a result.

Horror stories exist about people who made credit card purchases and allowed the accumulation of penalties, fees, and interest charges to push them toward bankruptcy, even though they might not have made any additional purchases. You need to understand that credit card debt is the most dangerous form of debt because it is easy to get but hard to escape once you lose control. If you want to take charge of your money, you must take strict control of your use of credit cards. Learn to hate debt more than you love the things that debt buys for you.

Annual and Other Fees

Credit card companies know that you'll be a great source of revenue if you use their cards and then aren't very well disciplined with your money. But if you use your card only occasionally and pay your balance in full each month, their ability to take your money is dramatically curtailed. For that reason, some cards have annual fees. That's what you're charged for the privilege of using the card, even though the merchant you do business with is also paying a fee for the transaction. Many cards have eliminated the annual fee, so look for one that doesn't include it.

There are many other fees associated with credit cards that you should know about. Cash advance fees are charges for taking cash from your credit account. When you do that, you will likely be charged a flat fee as well as interest on your full account balance. So if you have $3,000 in purchases and you withdraw $100 in cash, you will pay interest on the full $3,100. Other fees include telephone payment fees, balance transfer fees, and over-limit fees. You may say to yourself that a small fee here or there won't really hurt you, but those little charges add up very quickly. It's a bit like getting nibbled to death by a duck—each bite doesn't hurt that much, but you'll end up dead nevertheless!

Cars

Do you know how many people drive new cars? Nobody! The moment that car leaves the dealer's lot, it becomes a used car. In fact, look at the mileage on that new car on the lot and you'll often see that it's been driven more than around the block. Nevertheless, you're bombarded daily by messages of urgency and enticements to bring in your used car and exchange it for the dealer's used car. Let's look at some of the money traps that you'll find in the car business.

Sign and Drive

Once again, we see a variation of the old message: Get it now without paying anything. Car dealers dress up the message by saying that sign-and-drive is for smart shoppers who believe they've purchased a car within their budget and simply desire to roll all the costs—including taxes, bank fees, and dealer fees—into the overall car loan. This results in a higher monthly payment, but that's okay since it fits within the buyer's budget. Never mind that you're now financing your sales tax over five or more years—you can afford it.

The reality is that this message isn't geared toward prudent shoppers who have calculated the costs and determined that this is the best course of action. This message appeals to those who want a new car and don't have enough money to pay even the up-front fees, much less a down payment that would drop their overall cost of purchase.

Stay away from sign-and-drive if you want to take control of your money! If you need to finance your car, try to pay as much as possible up front. A car is a very emotional purchase. You get to pick the color, the interior, and the amazing sound system. Remember what we said about your emotions? They can be your enemy, and this is one area where you need to steel yourself against that enemy. Your feel-good attitude when you drive off the dealer's lot will evaporate very quickly when the reality of your financial decision hits you if you elect to sign and drive.

Zero Down

There's never been a better time for people with bad credit to drive the car they've always wanted!

When we saw this advertisement recently, our first thought was, "Are you kidding me?!" This is a direct appeal to people in financial trouble to get into even more financial trouble. Does anyone else think this kind of solicitation should be criminal? They're recognizing that you have credit trouble, and they're going to do what they can to add more debt to your burden. And they're doing this by appealing to your desire to drive the car you've "always wanted."

If you want to take control of your money, put off driving the car you've always wanted and drive the car you can afford now. That allows you to rebuild your credit more quickly. Then, after you've taken control of your finances, you can get the car you've always wanted and you'll pay a lot less for it. If you have bad credit, you need to address the issues that resulted in your bad credit. Just because you can afford the payments on that new car doesn't mean you should accept that obligation.

Zero-down offers are another variation of pulling you into the dealership, since you don't have to have money in your pocket. The fine print on many of these offers, though, is that zero down doesn't include taxes and other fees, which could amount to a couple thousand dollars or more. Again, the offer isn't designed to altruistically save you money. It's designed to separate you from your money with the reward of a shiny new car.

Upside-Down Car Loans

Do you remember being upside down when you were a kid? That might have been fun if you were hanging from a tree branch by your legs. What does *upside down* really mean? It means that what's up is down, and vice versa. It means that things aren't in the right order.

If you're upside down in your car loan, that means that you now own a car that is worth less than what you have left to pay on it. This might be the result of a high-interest loan, a rapidly depreciating car, or an overall bad deal at the initial purchase. Whatever the case, if you sold your car now the sale wouldn't bring in enough for you to pay off your loan. As with hanging by your legs as a kid, this isn't the way things should be.

Upside-down car loans are offered to get you to buy a new car, even if your current car isn't worth what you owe on it. This message sounds like a great deal because you get out of your current upside-down loan by buying a new car, and now you have a new car and a new payment. However, you need to understand that you're not getting out of the upside-down loan through the goodness of the dealer's heart. You're simply adding your outstanding balance to the new loan and consolidating two loans into one.

Here's how it works. Your old car is worth $15,000, but you still owe $20,000 on the loan. That means you're upside down by $5,000. So you go out and buy a new $30,000 car and use your current car as a trade-in. The dealer gives you the $15,000 credit and closes your $20,000 loan. Then you drive off the lot with a $30,000 car and a $35,000 loan. They'll add the $5,000 upside-down amount to the $30,000 financing for the new car. How many times do you think you can pull this off before the dealer decides that you're on your own?

Low-APR Loans

The APR is the cost of your loan. It tells you how much interest you're paying for the money you borrow. On the surface, a low APR sounds like a plus. And on the surface, it is. It's not the low APR that's the problem here, it's the way the low APR is marketed to you.

Which would you rather have if you're buying a car: (1) a $10,000 five-year loan at 5 percent or (2) a $12,000 seven-year loan at 3 percent? The 5 percent loan will have a monthly payment of around $189 and a total cost of around $11,300. The 3 percent loan will have a monthly payment of around $159 and a total cost of around $13,300. So although the second loan has a lower APR, the initial cost and the longer loan term still make it a more expensive choice.

The other danger with low-APR loan offers is that they have fairly strict qualifications attached to them. Your credit score needs to be in the top range in order to qualify for the advertised rate. This is usually not discussed until you've already done your shopping and have settled on a car. You go into the office and wait, while the salesperson runs the paperwork and checks your application. Shortly thereafter, the finance manager casually strolls over and informs you that they would love to be able to give you the advertised APR but your credit score is too low. You may have even checked your score with one of the major credit-reporting services, but this dealer uses another service to determine your eligibility. At this point, they're counting on you to not do the one thing you should do: walk out. You've invested too much time and energy in selecting your dream car, and they're selling you a convincing line about how they can get you to the monthly payment that you need. Never mind that it may mean adding several more years to your loan term. You begin to control your money when you control your actions in situations just like this.

$100 below Factory Invoice

This advertising catch line wants you to think that the dealers are willing to claim you as a dependent on their taxes next year because they graciously sold you a vehicle at a loss. You actually paid $100 less than the big window sticker said the car was worth. In every business and industry, sellers decide how much they really want to sell an item for and then mark the "retail" price higher so that they can advertise a discounted sale price. If you open a lemonade stand and you want to sell a glass for $1, all you need to do is make a big sign that says "$5 lemonade—only $1 today!"

Let's face it, car dealers are in business to make money just like everyone else. They are not going to pay the window invoice price for a vehicle and then sell it to you for $100 less than what they paid. First of all, the fine print in many of these advertisements tells you that the "factory invoice may not reflect actual dealer cost." Well then, what's the purpose of the factory invoice? That's their $5 lemonade sign.

Beyond that, you have to watch for dealer-installed accessories. The have factory invoice might be for $25,000, but the dealer has added $500 rust protection, $2,500 custom wheels, and a $1,500 audio upgrade. That's a total of $29,500, and you get that for

$29,400—$100 under invoice. The dealer profit on the extra $4,500 is enough to let them smile as you walk out the door.

Guaranteed Trade-in Allowance

You've almost certainly seen the advertisements telling you that the car dealer will you give $5,000 for your old vehicle, regardless of condition. If you're driving around in a clunker that has 200,000 miles and a used car value below $300, you might think that you can't believe your luck. You've found a dealer who will give you $5,000 for your car, and it's practically worthless! It's worth it to buy a new car just so you can get paid too much for your old car, right?

Wrong! This is a variation of the upside-down car loan. A dealer who is going to take a loss on one hand will find a way to make it up with interest on the other hand. The fact is, you could walk into the dealership with a crayon drawing of a car and they'd give you the trade-in credit. In fact, they might prefer that over the clunker, since the disposal costs are lower.

If you want to buy a car and you have a car to sell, you are responsible for two transactions, not one. You should first negotiate your best deal on the car you wish to purchase. After settling on a price, you can negotiate the trade-in deal. You then decide whether it's better to let the dealer take the car as a trade-in or whether you should sell it yourself. Part of the consideration, of course, is the time, energy, and money it will cost you to sell your car on your own. If you think you can sell your car for $2,000 and the dealer is willing to give you $1,200, you might decide that it would be worth the $800 to not have to go through the used-car selling process.

Homes and Real Estate

Refinance with Cash Back

Congratulations! You've been diligent in making your house payments, and you're slowly chipping away at your outstanding mortgage while building valuable equity in your home. The unscrupulous lenders see an opportunity to send you further into debt while taking their share of your hard-earned equity. They'll use terms like "get cash for that special occasion, take a vacation, or make home improvements." That last term is thrown in there to help convince you that you might actually put the cash back into your home. The fact remains that they're really trying to convince you that you have a real estate ATM from which you can make withdrawals and live your dreams.

One of the key points to remember about cashing out of your home equity is that most mortgages are thirty-year loans. Even though you might have a low interest rate, paying a principle balance over thirty years is not smart when that principle is used for consumer spending. If you take just $1,000 out of your home equity to purchase a vacation, at 7 percent annual interest that vacation will end up costing about $2,400. How much better it would be to leave the equity in your home and save an extra $1,000 so you can pay for that vacation with cash!

While it is true that people with high-interest debt could take cash from their homes and trade the high-interest debt for low-interest debt, this reduces the symptoms rather than removing the cause. That is, it looks good on the surface, but when the high-interest debt is lowered, many people eventually find themselves back in the same situation. Now they've taken cash out of their home to pay down their credit card debt, and they've subsequently built their credit card debt right back up again. Living on borrowed money is a behavior issue that must be retrained, and pulling cash out of your home is only a temporary fix. Besides, you're able to do that only once or twice before you've refinanced so many times that you have no more available equity to pull out with another refinance.

If you really want to take charge of your money, start looking at equity as a good thing to have, not a pool of funds to spend. Your home mortgage is usually a low-interest loan and the payments are smaller since they're spread over thirty years, but it is still debt. And you need to reduce and eliminate debt in order to truly have control over your finances.

No Closing Costs

You might be starting to see the pattern with these offers. They all sound great because that's how they get your attention. The wolf dresses in sheep's clothing because the sheep would have second thoughts about associating with a wolf in wolf's clothing. It has to look, sound, smell, and taste good to get your buy-in. The danger comes after you've swallowed the hook.

No-closing-cost loans are appealing because you have the chance to lower the interest rate on your mortgage without having to pay a lot of closing costs. The first point you should know is that these loans may be advertised as having no closing costs, but that doesn't necessarily mean that you won't have to pay anything at closing. There are other costs that may be collected, such as title searches, appraisals, and credit checks.

But even if you don't have to pay a dime at closing, these loans aren't necessarily the best financial choice. Whether the closing costs are rolled into the loan or not, the fact remains that there are costs associated with a mortgage loan closing. So why would lenders decide against charging those costs to you? Simple. They'll make it up in the interest rate, which means you're either paying now or paying later.

If you want to take charge of this aspect of your money, you need to consider how long you plan to be in your house and thus how long you will be paying the mortgage. If you have reason to believe that you'll have the mortgage for only a short time—say, less than a few years—then it may make sense to take a higher interest rate and avoid paying closing costs. On the other hand, there can be significant differences in interest rates between no-closing-cost loans and traditional loans. In that case, it may take only two or three years to make up the closing costs you had to pay up front, and then your loan is cheaper over the long haul.

Loan Points

Loan points are nothing more than prepaid interest. One point is equal to 1 percent of the value of your loan. So if you have a $250,000 mortgage, one point would cost you $2,500 at closing. Points are a little different from most of what we're talking about in this chapter in that they're not as much misleading as misunderstood.

The important decisions regarding whether or not to pay points at closing revolve around how long you expect to keep the loan and your tax situation. You must first consider how long you think you'll be paying on your loan. Since points are prepaid interest, you can expect a lower-interest-rate mortgage when you pay points. The more points you pay, the lower your interest rate goes. If you believe that you'll be in your house and paying the mortgage for many years, then paying points up front will eventually leave you with a lower overall loan expense. If you're in a business that moves you every two years, then you might want to pass on the points and take the higher interest rate.

The other consideration is the tax implication of paying points. We have to issue the caveat that everyone should consider current tax laws and your own financial situation. Having said that, points paid on your home mortgage have traditionally been tax deductible as home mortgage interest. Between the tax benefit and the lower mortgage interest rate, you may decide that points make sense for you.

Builder Upgrades

When you buy a new-construction home, you'll have the opportunity to customize certain aspects of your purchase. These can run the gamut of selections and might include upgraded carpeting, premium appliances, enhanced landscaping, and decorative fixtures and trim. Buying a home is exciting, and the emotions that are running rampant at that time may not put you in the best frame of mind for making sound decisions with your money. Furthermore, you'll be sorely tempted to not consider the true costs of various upgrades, since they'll all get wrapped into the loan and you'll only see a slight bump in your monthly payments. Here's a classic situation where you need to temper your emotional spending and do your best to keep your debt in check—even though it's home mortgage debt.

There are certainly cases in which it makes sense to have the builder add some extras to your home. Adding plumbing for a future bathroom or prewiring fixtures or audio systems is often much more economical during construction than afterward. You also need to consider the convenience factor of including carpet or trim upgrades before you move all your furniture into the house. Each of these considerations should be examined on its own merit, and you need to consider the cost of having the builder perform the work versus hiring a contractor later.

Remember that we're talking about taking charge of your money, not maximizing the amount of house you purchase for your mortgage. If you can't afford the monthly payment or if you're carrying a lot of credit card debt, you should pass on even good deals in order to avoid additional debt. You might be getting a great deal on the stainless steel dishwasher and refrigerator, but the basic enamel-coated appliance will get the job done and won't cost you any extra. A few years down the road, after you've paid off those credit cards, you can save up for the latest and greatest appliances. When you walk into the appliance store and pay cash for your upgrades, you'll go home with the satisfaction of knowing that you did it the smart way!

You should also be aware that builders sometimes offer upgrades that really aren't such good deals. In such cases, they're counting on you to succumb to your emotions and take the additional monthly payment to satisfy your dreaming. The builder knows that a $5,000 upgrade is viewed as small compared to a $250,000 mortgage. That same $5,000 charge, when considered by itself a few years later, appears a lot bigger. It's a matter of scale. If they can sell you on the fact that $5,000 is only a 2 percent increase to your $250,000 mortgage, you'll be much more inclined to spend freely. As Senator Everett Dirksen once said, "A billion here, a billion there. Pretty soon it adds up to real money." The point is that even a billion dollars can seem like a small amount if it's compared against something much bigger. Take Senator Dirksen's quote to heart for your finances: "A hundred here, a hundred there. Pretty soon it adds up to real money!"

Adjustable Rate Mortgages (ARMs)

Adjustable rate mortgages (ARMs) are loans that have a lower initial interest rate than a fixed-rate loan. The lower-rate period is generally between one and three years. After the initial period expires, the loan rate is adjusted based on current market rates. The adjustment may go up or down, and there is a limit on how much the rate can change.

There is nothing intrinsically wrong with ARMs if you understand the details of the loan and you have good financial discipline. If you know that you will be in your home for only a few years, a five-year ARM may save you money because you'll be selling the home before the loan has a chance to adjust higher.

One of the problems with ARMs, though, is that there are so many combinations of initial rate periods, adjustment caps, lifetime adjustments, and prepayment penalties. A standard thirty-year fixed home loan has enough details in it to keep you on your toes when you fill out the paperwork. Complicated ARM loans are all but impossible to thoroughly comprehend. Borrowers often don't find out about the dangerous fine print until they get hit with a rate increase that they can't meet.

The second and bigger issue with ARMs is that they draw borrowers in with teasingly low interest rates. People buy homes they really can't afford because the ARM lets them manage the payments for a short time. In fact, some loans are actually negative-amortization loans—that is, you pay less than the minimum interest payment, so your outstanding balance actually grows from month to month! Borrowers look at the monthly payment with the ARM and stretch to buy a house they can barely afford. The first time the rate adjusts upward, they've exceeded their budget and they fall into debt or foreclosure.

Retail Shopping

The dangers and traps that exist in the retail world are not necessarily worse than in some of the areas we've already discussed. However, because you spend a lot more time on retail shopping than you do shopping for cars and houses, you need to be especially on your guard against the tricks and manipulations in the retail world.

Rebates

We'll start with one of the worst offenders on the shelves of stores everywhere. Rebates have the image of being the best part of shopping: Spend money; get money back! But you need to recognize that the downside of rebates usually outweighs the benefits for the average consumer.

A rebate is a refund that you get from the store or manufacturer when you purchase an item. Let's assume you go shopping for a new cell phone. One model catches your eye, and the price—in big numbers—is $99. When you look at the fine print, it says "after $100 manufacturer rebate." In one fell swoop, the store has convinced you that you're paying $99 when you are, in fact, paying $199. Paying $199 and getting $100 back is not the same as paying $99. If they wanted you to pay only $99, why not just drop the price to $99 instead of forcing you to jump through their hoops to collect your own money back? The store will argue that it's more efficient to have short-term promotions through rebates than to drop and raise prices directly. Besides, price increases—even when they follow price drops—are rarely looked upon favorably by consumers. So a rebate allows the store to keep the retail price of $199 and then use rebate promotions whenever they wish. The price always stays at $199, but the rebate dictates when you get the additional $100 discount.

Now let's look at rebate reality. First of all, you don't get the rebate unless you file for it within the allotted time. It won't do you any good to take the rebate form home and leave it on your desk until the filing expiration date. Miss the filing, miss the money. If you eliminate the number of shoppers who never file the rebate form, the manufacturer is left with a small enough obligation to make the rest of the process worthwhile. If only one out of four shoppers submits the $100 rebate form, the actual cost to the manufacturer is only $25. That means the manufacturer collects an average of $174 per unit sold, not the advertised $99.

Second, most rebates require that you cut out the bar code, sign your name with your middle initial, and submit the thumbprint of your firstborn male. Miss one step and the rebate is considered incomplete and, therefore, not payable. The instructions for the various hoops they want you to jump through are usually printed in small type at the bottom of a receipt that's only slightly shorter than a double roll of bath tissue. It's fully expected that a certain percentage of people will zig when they should have zagged. That takes the manufacturer's obligation down even further.

Finally, we're assuming that all stores and manufacturers are as pure as the wind-driven snow and will actually pay the rebate if you follow their instructions. That's simply not the case. How many times have you received a rebate check in a nondescript envelope and almost tossed it out as junk mail? Do you think that's not part of the plan? If you do everything right and then fail to cash the check, the rebate is as good as not paid. On top of that, there are more than a few companies that delay payment for a long period or simply refuse to honor a valid rebate request. They delay payment because they understand that time is money. The longer they keep your money, the more they have and the less you have. If that doesn't make you angry, then you're not paying attention.

If you want to take charge of your money, then you need to consider a rebate as a bonus. Definitely submit the form and make every attempt to collect your money, but compare prices based on cash out of your pocket. When comparing prices, a $199 item with a $100 rebate is not a $99 item.

Open a Charge Account, Get a Discount

Hey, you can't blame stores for wanting to get you to add their charge cards to your wallet. If you have a store charge card, then you'll be more inclined to take your business there. That's especially true if they offer you discounts and other enticements to continue using the cards. They also recognize that they have a much greater ability to market directly to you when they know your contact information and buying habits. If they know how to find you and what your hot buttons are, they have the advantage. They would much prefer to have control over your money.

The positive side of opening a store charge account is that you often receive a nice discount for your initial purchase. If you're buying a big-ticket item, it might be worth opening that charge account for the possible hundreds of dollars in savings. But in order to make this work for you so that you can take charge of your money, you need to know how to use it properly.

If you're just opening the account for that big-ticket discount, then make sure you can pay the balance in full when you get the bill. If you don't pay the balance in full, you have another high-interest credit card that's adding to your family debt. Once you've paid the balance off, cut up the card and close the account. Don't throw the card away, since it could expose you to identity theft. And don't assume that the account is harmless if you don't use it anymore. Get rid of the card and get rid of the account.

Twelve Months Same as Cash

This financial evil takes many forms, but nowhere is it as direct as in the retail business. As we pointed out in the discussion of zero-APR first-year credit cards, this works if you're disciplined and you pay the balance in full by the end of the twelve-month grace period. But the reality is that many people aren't disciplined and able to pay, and this becomes a trap for spending money they don't have.

"Twelve months same as cash" is designed purely to get you to make a purchase now when you should be waiting to make the purchase later. If retailers thought that everyone would pay the balance in full, what would be their motivation in loaning you the money for twelve months? The motivation lies in the additional revenue that comes from the finance and penalty fees that will eventually be collected. Along with that, every retailer knows that a sale today is worth more than a sale tomorrow.

Buy Two, Get One Free

Admit it. You have walked out of a convenience store with a 64-ounce fountain drink just because it was only twenty cents more than the 48-ounce drink, right? Both choices are tantamount to sidling up to a tanker filled with diet soda, and you know that it's highly unlikely that your bladder will support either decision. Nevertheless, you were drawn in by the perceived value of going with the larger selection.

Buying more than you need is a common fault that often begins with good intentions but ends with wasted money. Getting value from quantity purchases is actually a smart and thrifty idea if you are able to utilize the full quantity. Bulk warehouse stores fuel an entire industry that is built on the premise that you'll find a use for bushel-sized boxes of cornflakes. If you can find a way to keep and eventually consume large quantities or multiple purchases, then economies of scale really do play in your favor.

The danger that you have to avoid is buying more than you need or buying something you *don't* need. Let's say you're on a trip and you find that you didn't pack a necessary pair of dress socks. You have more than enough socks at home, but none with you. You walk into a store and see that you can buy one pair of socks for $10 or get three pairs for $25. Clearly, buying three pairs gives you a much lower price per pair than buying the single pair. But if you have no need for anything more than the one missing pair of socks, then you've ultimately ended up spending two and a half times what you should have spent. The value would have made the three pairs a good choice only if you had need of three pairs.

Although the sock example seems pretty harmless on the surface, consider how many ways this hits your pocketbook:

- Too many cell phone minutes in your prepaid plan
- Three cases of soda when you planned to buy only one
- Two sport jackets since the second was half off
- Sandwich, chips, and drink when you just wanted a snack

Still not entirely convinced of the pervasiveness of this marketing ploy? Type "Buy 1 Get 1 Free" into your favorite online search site and see how many results come up.

Gift Cards

Store gift cards are truly the gift that keeps on giving—to the store. In 2006, the value of unused gift cards was estimated to be over $8 billion! When you purchase a gift card, the store immediately receives your money and waits for you to redeem the credit. These cards seem like a handy way to avoid having to do the shopping. Why not let your friend choose her own gift, after all? Actually, there are a number of reasons why you shouldn't.

First, a gift card is just like cash. If you lose it, it's gone forever from your account. But if you lose it, it's pure profit for the retailer. Not bad, from the retailer's perspective. Either you spend the money and the store gets its normal margins, or you lose the card and the store gets the entire amount. If you buy a gift from a retailer and include the gift receipt, your friend can return the gift and get a store credit equal to the value of a gift card. The difference is that a handbag is a lot harder to misplace under the car seat.

Second, many gift cards have expiration dates and nonuse fees. You decide to give a $100 mall gift card to your favorite niece, since you don't want to limit her to a specific store. She's busy and doesn't use the card for ten months. What she doesn't realize is that the card has a $2.50 per month nonuse fee. When she finally goes shopping, she's shocked to find out that her $100 card is now worth $75. Worse yet, if she had waited a few more months and the card had expired, she would have thrown away the entire $100.

Gift cards may not hit your pocketbook, since you're giving away the $100 whether the recipient gets to spend it or not. But that misses the point. You rightfully want to give a gift and have the recipient enjoy the full value. Why make it harder for the receiver to take advantage of your generosity? Instead of a gift card, give cash or a check. Sure, it's not as pretty as a fancy card, but cash doesn't expire or erode with time. People are a lot less inclined to misplace cash, and if a check is lost, you can always write a new one. As an alternative, take your best shot at a gift and include the receipt. If it turns out to be a white elephant, let your friend return the gift and enjoy shopping with the store credit.

Too Many Cards

It's far too easy to fill out an application and get a credit card. Just about anyone in business with consumers can have a branded credit card issued for you. Here's just a short list of the businesses that want your credit as well as your sales:

- Airlines
- Department stores

- Gas stations
- Furniture stores
- Hotels
- Phone companies

The list is really endless—everyone wants you to take their credit cards, and they'll offer you all sorts of enticements. Credit cards in and of themselves are not dangerous, but too many cards can create unexpected problems, which, in turn, keep you from taking charge of your money now.

A large number of open accounts drag down your credit score. Even if you don't use the accounts, each time you apply for a new account, it registers as an inquiry on your credit report. Too many inquiries, and your score starts to drop. When you follow through and open the account, your available credit line increases and further affects your credit score. Use the cards recklessly, and you'll find yourself paying interest and penalties on large credit card balances—and then your credit score drops even further. Why should you be concerned about your credit score? Because the lower your score, the higher the interest you have to pay on loans and charges.

A second danger in having too many open charge accounts is the temptation to spend money that you don't really have. If you have one credit card with a $5,000 credit limit, you've limited your debt temptation to $5,000. Add two retail store cards to that lineup, with $3,000 credit limits on each, and you now have $11,000 of possible spending. You don't have any more money than you started with, but you do have a lot more potential debt.

The third danger is that every open credit card account is a potential target for identity theft. Do you open each credit card statement and reconcile the charges against your receipts every month? You should. If you're not doing that with one or two cards, how will you manage to keep up with five or ten cards?

Get Angry and Get Control

Taking charge of your money means knowing where it comes from and where it's going. If you have a blind spot about your spending, you won't be able to control of your finances. If you don't recognize the forces arrayed against you, however subtle, you'll continue to be a victim. Now that we've alerted you to some of the many ways in which companies try to play your emotions like a fiddle, you are empowered to equip yourself for battle. That's right. You're going into battle with those who want to control your money for you. Decide now that you will take charge of your money and then make it happen!

PART THREE

The Strategy

Chapter 7

Create a Family Budget

Your financial plan is your best accountability partner. Your plan will remain firm and emotionless, keeping you in check when your own emotions try to steer you off course.

One of the most important exercises that you can undertake is the creation of a family budget. The family budget is the core document of your financial discipline. This budget is as important to a single woman living alone as it is to parents with five kids. There is no age limit—young or old—for creating and using a family budget. This document is crucial because it functions as your road map for income, expenses, debts, and your goals. Everything that we discuss in this book and the accompanying workbook can be wrapped together into a budget.

This task can be so daunting that many people never even attempt it. Take comfort in knowing that there is no right or wrong with a budget. Any effort toward structuring your finances is better than no effort. Furthermore, you always have the latitude to refine your plan as you learn and grow.

To help you get started, this chapter is organized according to key principles that you can apply to your family budget. Think of them as gold nuggets: You are rich when you have a handful of them, but, applied individually, each one makes you a little bit richer as well. Let's begin by looking at the components that make up a useful family budget.

Keep It Super Simple

The hallmark of a good plan is simplicity. You can prepare forms and checklists, require expense accounting from everyone in the family, and track your monthly income and projections in a dozen ways. The fact is that if you spend endless hours refining the perfect plan, it will probably be too complex to execute.

We are strong advocates of the KISS principle: Keep It Super Simple. A simple plan is easy to create and easy to execute. Both qualities are necessary if you're going to make a family budget that will actually have an impact on your behavior and allow you to take charge of your money. As we go through the mechanics of developing a family budget, you'll notice that the action steps we suggest adhere to this core principle.

Set Your Goals

When you create any kind of plan, it is assumed that you have an end objective that you're working toward. This is true with your family budget as well. Simply listing your income and expenses might make for an interesting exercise, but it doesn't give you a direction for improving your situation. We're guessing that your broad goal is to take charge of your money, but to get there you have to take small steps along the way. You need to create your own milestones in order to track your progress and recognize that the goal of taking control of your money is within your reach.

Follow the first key concept when you set your goals: Keep it super simple. Don't make the goals too complicated or set them so far beyond reach that you won't see any progress. As with every other part of your budget, you can add or eliminate goals along the way to better reflect your family's priorities and circumstances at the time. For example, you might have set an initial goal to completely eliminate your student loan debt within two years. But then your child becomes seriously ill, and that leaves you with a large credit card debt. In this case, you should go ahead and change your goal from retiring your student loan debt to retiring your credit card debt. As your circumstances change, set new goals with new deadlines, and move forward from there.

When you sit down to set your goals, you might not be sure where to begin. What if you have so many goals that you can't determine a starting point? No problem. Pick any three income issues and any three expense issues, and use them as your initial goals. Don't worry whether they are the most important three; that's not what counts here. The crucial point is that you start, and eventually you will refine your budget so that it is helping you take charge of your money.

Try a Kit

When was the last time you hand-rolled pizza dough, tossed it into the air and caught it, ladled the sauce, scattered the cheese, and popped open your brick oven? Unless you actually own a pizza shop, chances are that you've never gone through that process in order to enjoy a hot pizza. Most likely, the closest you've come is fumbling the frozen pie as you unwrapped the plastic, accidentally tossing it into the air, and making a saving catch before it hits the floor.

Having something prepared and ready to go is often good and even necessary. The same holds true for your family budget. We're not advocating that you reinvent the wheel through your own trial-and-error process. There are many prepackaged budget kits on the market today that let you plug in your own information and generate a basic personalized budget. They often have very useful analysis features to help you identify where your money is going and may include helpful suggestions about ways to improve your budget that you might not have considered on your own. It's a bit like having a personal budget coach right there with you.

Don't abrogate your responsibilities to the budget-in-a-box, however. It is simply a tool to help you take charge of your money. You still have to do the work and make the decisions. Spend a little time shopping for the right kit—they're not all created equal. Check out the reputation of the firm or individual offering the kit, and scrutinize them as carefully as you would your financial or tax advisor.

Discipline Beats Brains

Don't get us wrong here: You need to learn the basic steps, strategies, and principles involved in managing your money. It's important that you know some of the terminology related to money, such as *time value, corporate bonds,* and *credit limits.* It's also important that you are aware of financial practices and strategies such as margin investing and portfolio diversification. When all is said and done, though, the people who are most successful with their money are not always the brightest in the bunch. Rather, the people who exercise the most discipline are the ones who cross the finish line as winners.

Being smart does not automatically translate into being disciplined. We're sure that if you look around you will see some very bright individuals who have dug themselves into a financial pit. In fact, news reports are filled with stories about financial professionals who have taken big hits and lost control of their own money—or that of others! The failure of these professionals probably doesn't have to do nearly as much with their intellect as it does with their follow-through. If you gave them a quiz, they would have all the right answers. The problem lies in their ability to do what they very well know they should do.

With that in mind, you now have the opportunity to position yourself in the upper echelon of money managers. Starting with your own money, you can commit to handling your finances with steady discipline. Although that may sound like a simple task—and it is—it's not an *easy* task. Your emotions will fight you every step of the way. You'll have to make some tough choices once in a while. The reward for your steadfastness is that you will become one of the few to reach the envied position of being in control of your money. If that's what you're driving toward, then take heart in that fact; you have the knowledge, and you choose the discipline. It's all there for the taking—so take it!

Everyone Participates

A family budget isn't worth the paper it's written on if only part of the family is on board. This is most acutely true for the husband and wife—you two are a team. One of you cannot relegate the budget responsibility to the other and then expect to make it all work. Of course, one of you may have a greater role in creating the actual budget and making sure everyone sticks to the plan. However, both of you must have a part in setting the goals and priorities. Your family history might be such that one spouse handled all the money issues: checkbooks, investments, accounting, and taxes. That's fine, and you don't necessarily need to change that approach. But you do need to collaborate on the budget and the way it will be applied to the day-to-day finances.

Don't exclude the kids from this process, either. This also extends to other members of the household. Families these days do not exclusively consist of Mom, Dad, and the kids. The Sandwich Generation includes Mom and Dad with the kids and their grandparents under the same roof. You might have a niece living with you while she's attending a local college. Whatever the situation, you need to include everyone who is contributing to either income or expenses. If you have a monthly budget for utilities, it doesn't help your cause to have your long-lost cousin running the air-conditioning at a level that turns your home into a meat locker. Let everyone know what the budget priorities are and the role they can play in ensuring the plan's success.

Write It Down

In the world of professional trading, you can use a *stop order* to help protect your trade in the event that the market moves against you and you start to lose money. A stop order automatically sells your stock if the stock price falls, and it works great as long as it has, in fact, been entered by the trader. The problem is that many inexperienced traders never actually place a stop order with their broker. They have an exit price in mind and tell themselves that if the stock drops to their exit price, they'll get out and limit their losses. We refer to this as a "mental stop order"—it's an order that exists only in the trader's mind.

Can you guess what the main difference is between stop orders and mental stop orders? Stop orders are executed all the time, while mental stop orders are rarely executed. More times than not, if the stock price drops to the exit price that the trader has in mind, either he will forget to enter his order or he'll come up with justifications for holding on just a little longer. Inevitably, the trader loses much more with a mental stop order than he would have with a true stop order. Having good intentions of doing something with your money is not the same as actually doing it!

The same rule also applies to your family budget. If you're serious about taking control of your finances, you need to have a written plan. It's too easy to conveniently forget about the details if you try to keep the plan in your head. You'll fall into all of the same traps as the trader, including coming up with seemingly valid reasons why you shouldn't stick to your plan when the going gets tough. Your plan is your accountability partner, holding you to your goals and priorities even when your emotions are steering you off course.

A Budget Is a Marathon, Not a Sprint

A marathon and a sprint are two completely different races. A marathon is a long-distance race covering twenty-six miles, while a sprint may be as short as one hundred meters. Sprinters can go all out because the distance is so short. Sprinters have no need to pace themselves or keep any energy in reserve. Their finish line comes up quickly, and they abandon everything else to reach it as quickly as possible.

Marathon runners can't afford to burn up their energy early in the race. Although it may be impressive to take off like a bullet from the starting line, marathoners know that giving it all they've got at the start almost guarantees that they won't have enough left to cross the finish line. Marathoners have to plan for several hours, not several seconds or minutes.

Your work with your family budget is much more like preparing for and running a marathon than a sprint. You have to commit to working through this process for years. Don't expect to wave a magic budget wand over your finances and find that they're in perfect order. If you stopped a marathoner in the middle of a race and asked her how she was feeling, she might tell you that she hurts and she'd really like to quit now. So why doesn't she? She presses on because the rewards of crossing the finish line are greater than the pain of the race. Your budget can affect you the same way. You might run into situations that make you feel like you're just ready to quit. Don't! Stick with your plan and press onward, because your reward at the finish line is knowing that you really have taken charge of your money.

Review Often

Your family budget should be a living, breathing document. Unlike the Ten Commandments given to Moses, your budget is not etched into stone tablets. You have the option—or, rather, the *obligation*—to review your budget frequently and make adjustments as necessary to reach your goals and objectives. You will likely find that you're a lot better equipped to deal with your finances after reading *Take Charge of Your Money Now!* You'll be able to look back to the time when you weren't nearly as knowledgeable about finances and see how far you've come. That learning process will continue, and next year you'll be even better equipped to fine-tune your budget.

Because you don't have perfect knowledge and experience now, you should make sure your budget develops and improves along with your skills. It is not necessary to tweak the budget too often. Unless there are extenuating financial circumstances, you should review your budget about twice a year. This is not so frequent that you end up making extra work for yourself, but it is still frequent enough to allow for helpful improvements.

Here's a good checklist of items to review in your family budget:

- What new income streams have been added?
- What income streams have dropped out or been reduced?
- What new income opportunities have you identified?
- What expenses have been added?
- What expenses have changed—higher or lower?
- What debts have you retired?
- What new liabilities have been added?
- How well are your record keeping and accounting working? How might you modify the way you handle these activities to give you better or more timely information?
- Are your time frames reasonable or do they need adjustment?
- Are your goals still appropriate for your family?
- How well are your investments and savings performing? Take this opportunity to rebalance and reallocate as necessary. For example, can you move some of your savings into a CD that pays a higher interest rate?

- Are you properly protecting your family's finances? Review your insurance needs as part of this budget review.

Remember that the budget review is designed to keep you on the right track. Changes to your budget should improve your level of control and discipline. When you review and fine-tune your budget, keep the following question in mind: Will this change take me closer to my goals? Any changes that you make should ultimately lead you toward better control over your finances.

Become a Teacher

The best students of a new subject are those who attempt to teach others while they themselves are learning. If you can explain the key points of a budget to a friend, grandchild, or coworker, then you know that you're absorbing what's really important.

A word of caution here: Everyone's financial situation is different, so be prepared to share concepts, not details. If you decide to reduce your health insurance expenses by assuming a high deductible, that's your business. Doing the same thing may or may not make sense for the friend with whom you're sharing your budget ideas. As we've seen in this chapter, the following basic principles are universally applicable:

- Keep it super simple.
- Set your goals.
- Try a kit.
- Discipline beats brains.
- Everyone participates.
- Write it down.
- A budget is a marathon not a sprint.
- Review often.
- Become a teacher.

These are the key concepts that you should focus on as you help someone else with a budget plan. Certainly, share ideas that work for you, and suggest improvements along the way. Just be aware that your family budget is as unique and designed to meet the needs of your individual family as your own home.

The family budget section of the workbook takes you step-by-step through the process of creating a budget. Don't worry about getting every piece of information exactly right at this stage. You'll have ample opportunity to review and adjust your budget along the way. For now, just commit to getting started and know that you're embarking on a journey of empowerment. You're on the road that leads to taking control of your money now!

Chapter 8

Keep It Super Simple

The simplest may not be the most impressive, but it is often the most achievable. It is far better to succeed in simplicity than to fail with a grandiose plan.

At what point in your life did things start to get complicated? Can you remember the days when you were a child and your carefree attitude allowed you to go with the flow? Most of us can look back and find at least one chapter in our lives during which things seemed easy and stress free.

Go to a park or a playground and observe the children running about. You will find that they possess a certain energy and innocence that is refreshing to watch. Kids have a way of making life look so easy. You may have seen your own children, grandchildren, or nieces and nephews display this type of happy-go-lucky behavior.

One of the most amazing things about younger children is the way they communicate. Some struggle with their sentences or, at the very least, mispronounce a word or two along the way. If you listen to them carefully, you will notice how direct and simple their thought process is. It is most noticeable right before they make you laugh. If they want something, they ask for it. If they have an opinion about someone, they just blurt it out. If something is bothering them, they don't keep it to themselves, however much you wish they sometimes would!

The question is, at what point do our lives get so complicated? Somewhere along the way we bought into the idea that more is better. More clothes, more food, bigger cars, and, of course, more money. With every new thing we add to our lives we increase not only our stress levels but also our risk levels.

You might ask how stress levels are elevated by having more things. Consider that more clothes require bigger closets. More food leads to the need for bigger clothes! Having a bigger, more expensive car now requires that you park all the way down at the end of the parking lot to avoid the door dings left by people who couldn't care less about your fancy automobile. This, by the way, is what's happening outside in the mall parking lot while you are busy shopping for those bigger clothes. As trivial as it might sound, those little door dings in life keep adding up until gradually you have left your happy-go-lucky childhood ways behind and ended up in the realm of not-so-happy-and-lucky adulthood.

Lower Your Stress

According to the Consumer Federation of America (CFA), money worries are among the most common sources of personal and family stress. In addition to this, financial stress takes an emotional and physical toll that can contribute to sleepless nights, backaches, headaches, and even life-threatening diseases such as high blood pressure and heart disease.

Someone once said that wedding cake was the leading cause of divorce, but, in reality, money pressure is the leading cause of marital breakups. It is true that money cannot buy happiness, but lack of money can surely put a wrench into a happy marriage. If you find yourself in a position where your credit card balances are soaring or you are constantly arguing with your partner over nickels and dimes, here are some steps you can take to relieve some of the pressure:

- **FOCUS ON THE THINGS YOU HAVE RATHER THAN THE THINGS YOU ARE LACKING.**

    Take inventory of what you possess. Include the material things like your home and car, but don't forget to leave out the things that count the most, like your health and relationships.

- **GET RID OF THE CLUTTER THAT'S AROUND YOU.**

    Throwing out the things you don't need can be a cleansing experience. Go into that attic and look around the house for things that get in the way. Hold a yard sale or donate them to charity. By the way, you can deduct such donations on your taxes if you take these possessions to a charitable organization or church. After you have gotten rid of the excess, organize the possessions you have left, and you will discover that less is more.

- **TAKE CARE OF YOURSELF AND GET BACK IN SHAPE.**

    Regardless of age, exercise is one of the best ways to relieve stress. It increases the level of oxygen to your brain, which gives you more energy and enables you to think more clearly. Clearing your mind and body results in a surge of energy that helps you win the battle against falling behind in your plan for financial success—and you'll look great, too.

- **EAT A BALANCED DIET.**

    This falls into the same category as the preceding point, and it could wind up being one of your biggest challenges. Remember that what you put into your body determines what you get out of it. A mule will eat anything, but a race car needs the right fuel blend.

Simplicity Is Perfection

A few years ago we were in Texas presenting a seminar to an audience of about three hundred people. The event was held at the beautiful Southfork Ranch, which is internationally renowned as the filming location for the *Dallas* television series. Everyone was having a great time as we presented our ideas about keeping it super simple.

We had a full day of presentations divided into four 90-minute sessions, and between each session we had breaks for people to grab a bite to eat, stretch their legs, and ask questions. Throughout the day one gentleman had his computer out on the corner of the stage, showing people his own strategy for trading the markets. A small crowd huddled around him as he proceeded to conduct his own mini seminar on the side. Curious, we walked over to see what all the commotion was about. As we approached, the "presenter" was kind enough to invite us to look at his system. Keep in mind that we had just stepped off the stage after giving a lengthy presentation on keeping it super simple in the markets.

When we looked at his computer screen we couldn't help laughing. There were charts and lines and technical indicators we had never seen before. We asked him to point out where the price was on the screen, and there was a long pause as even he had trouble finding the price line on the chart. By the way, if you didn't know this already, the price line is the most important line on any stock chart.

What most amazed us was not his total disregard for simplicity but rather the questions he drew from the crowd around him. It seems that people are inevitably drawn to the complicated. Our question to you is this: Do you want to create more questions for yourself or do you want answers that will help you reach your ultimate financial goals? If you are looking for answers, then do what you can to resist the temptation to overcomplicate things.

Your Checklist

Before any pilot even thinks about taking off, there is a checklist that must be followed to ensure that all safety measures are in place.

Engines working properly? Check.

Seatbelts on and securely fastened? Check.

Fuel? Check.

Develop your own daily or weekly checklist to make sure you are progressing in a direction that keeps you in line with the financial plan we talked about earlier. Such a checklist is more of a daily action plan to help you be more productive, not just with your money, but also with your time. Following is a sample of what this plan might look like. You can copy these points to your own checklist and/or add points that are tailored more to your needs:

- **START YOUR DAY WITH SOME QUIET TIME.**
  The busier your life is, the harder this will be for you, but it is important that you prepare your mind for the tasks at hand. Sit in a room quietly by yourself for about fifteen minutes and think about what you need to accomplish. If you are so inclined, this is also a good time to pray or meditate while you focus on your goals.

- **REVIEW YOUR FAMILY BUDGET.**
  It's also a good idea to start your day with a clear picture of where you stand with regard to your budget. You may want to do this on a weekly or biweekly basis.

- **PURCHASE WHAT YOU NEED, NOT WHAT YOU WANT.**
  Refrain from supersizing your purchases during the day. If you are under budget at the end of the month, you can then treat yourself to a reward for following your own rules for spending.

- **TRASH THE CREDIT CARD APPLICATIONS THAT COME IN THE MAIL.**
  Your popularity isn't measured by how many credit companies solicit your business; everyone gets them. If you really want to put them to good use, then save them in a container to burn in the fireplace during the winter months. The better thing to do is

to work on getting your name removed from one mailing list per week. This takes a little time, but it is worth it in the end. You might even save a tree or two in the process.

- **TAKE A WALK AFTER LUNCH.**
This not only helps you feel better, but it clears your mind of some of the things that distract you from your goals. Remember that good physical health leads to better fiscal health.

- **TRY TO SET ASIDE $10 A DAY IN CASH.**
Stash some cash. Surely this is not an exercise for getting rich quick; it is simply one that will help you in an emergency. Should you be faced with a short-term emergency such as a storm or a power outage, you can pull funds from your cash savings without having to worry about getting to a bank or cash machine.

- **TURN OFF THE TELEVISION, TURN ON THE TUNES, AND PICK UP A BOOK.**
If you are skeptical about what this point will do for you, then we challenge you to try it for twenty-one days. Purge the negative from your mind by turning off the tube and turn on some upbeat, positive music instead. And while you're listening, pick up a good book from time to time.

- **STAY ORGANIZED.**
Clutter breeds confusion. By organizing your calendar, your office, and your personal life, you will have an easier time finding things you need when you need them. This not only helps to relieve stress but also keeps you from wasting valuable time.

- **ADJUST YOUR GOALS.**
At the end of each day take a look back at what you have accomplished. Were you able to achieve everything you wanted to? If not, then add those items to the next day's list and prioritize. Make each goal S-M-A-R-T: Specific, Measurable, Attainable, Relevant, and Trackable. If your goals are too am-

bitious, you will wind up frustrated. You can always adjust your goals in order to reach them, but make sure you are not setting them too low. This would only cause you to stall or move backward. Review, revisit, revise, and renew your financial goals continuously.

Profits under Pressure

There are some professionals who handle money very well under pressure. Floor traders spend their careers in the pressure cooker known as the trading pit. The energy level is constantly redlining as traders scream and jostle for position in their attempts to buy and sell. What you may not realize is that the careers of many traders are short-lived. It's quite difficult to sustain this level of emotional and physical output and still make sound decisions about your money. There are some trading firms that actually pay for their traders to take vacations because a luxury cruise is cheaper than a bad trade.

Most people do not make the best financial decisions under pressure. This is one of the reasons that many financial experts recommend to clients who have lost a spouse that they wait a year before making any major financial decisions such as selling their home. Your mental state certainly affects the way you approach challenges in your life, so it's important for you to monitor your own thoughts in order to stay in peak mental condition.

Are you an optimist or a pessimist? A Harvard study followed the lives of ninety-nine students starting at age twenty-five and found that those who were optimists were significantly healthier at ages forty-five and sixty than those who were pessimists. Similar studies have shown that pessimism is a good predictor of poor physical and financial health, and if that's not enough, this group was more susceptible to infectious disease and early mortality. In other words, being a pessimist literally means that you will likely die sooner. It's interesting to note that if there is anything present in the trading pits, its supreme self-confidence and optimism. If you want to take charge of your money, you need to approach your finances with the same level of confidence and determination.

Take this journey one step at a time. Escape on a vacation when you feel the pressures mounting. Set aside some quiet time to reflect and plan. Stay fit and healthy while being thankful for your blessings. In the end, *keep it super simple* and take charge of your money now!

Chapter 9

Secrets of the Marketplace

Viewed from a distance, the porcupine could pass for a lovable pet. A closer inspection shows the quills ready to inflict pain and harm. The world of finance has its own porcupines. Get to know them before you reach for a mistake.

The hard truth is that most companies don't care about your financial state, and the last thing they are interested in is sharing their trade secrets with the general public. A company exists to capture market share and increase shareholder value. Your responsibility is to take charge of your money, whether that money is coming or going. On the outgoing side, how you spend your money sometimes presents a much greater challenge than how you acquire your money. Have you ever known someone who made a substantial income but always seemed to be on the edge of financial disaster? Their problem isn't income, it's spending.

Secret #1. The Profit Margin

Take a look at the bottled water industry. As children, we would have laughed at the thought of paying for bottled water in the supermarket. Who in their right mind would pay for anything that is so abundant and free for the taking? Well, somewhere along the way we have been convinced by the marketing messages that the water that comes out of our kitchen sinks is unhealthy. Not only have we been told that it is a bad thing to consume water from the tap, but we have been sold the idea that water is much healthier for us when taken from a spring located somewhere in the French Alps. You probably never thought about what you're actually paying for when you buy a bottle of water, so let's break that down for you. What's most obvious is the plastic bottle itself. Not only are you paying for the manufacture of the plastic bottle, but you are paying for the disposal of it as well. Dumping it at the landfill may not be something you pay for on the front end of your purchase, but you certainly pay for it on the back end, as disposal costs are ultimately passed on to consumers. What might be more surprising is the cost of shipping. If you are buying imported water, then you will be paying for shipping costs, as it travels by rail or sea thousands of miles before getting to the stores.

The hidden secret is in the profit margin per bottle of water. According to a report published by the nonprofit Earth Policy Institute, not only is bottled water no healthier than tap water, but it can be ten thousand times more expensive. Did you get that? Ten thousand times more expensive! It's no wonder the bottled water companies love you so much.

The financial industry is filled with high-profit-margin products that are being sold to you every day. We've already mentioned credit cards as money traps, but consider further the profit margin with those cards. If you miss one payment, you'll pay a late payment penalty along with interest. You will also see that your annual percentage rate increases due to the missed payment. Another popular high-profit-margin financial product is annuities. These are aggressively sold by financial salespeople because of their revenue to the salesperson more than their benefit for you. Annuities have high fees, surrender charges, and management expense. In fact, within the financial industry, the saying is that annuities are sold, not bought.

So the corporate secret highlighted in this example is this:

The general public is easily persuaded to make a purchase as long as enough money is pumped into a well-developed marketing campaign—especially if the message highlights ideas of good health, good taste, prosperity, and overall well-being for the individual consumer.

Secret #2. The Conditioned Response

Another common practice you should know about is the way commercial advertising campaigns target you. You are, in a sense, being programmed each and every day of your life. For instance, imagine it is ten o'clock at night and you are sitting on your sofa watching your favorite television program. Before you are able to get to your remote control to change the channel, you are captivated by a commercial showing the most delicious sandwich in the world. Although your original goal was to change the channel to avoid the commercial, your senses are charged with this new delight at precisely the same moment your stomach is growling, a reminder that dinner was a few hours ago.

Do you think the timing of that commercial was a random coincidence, or do you think there was a little bit more research done on the part of the advertising firm whose client they are promoting on the national airwaves? Food industries are fully aware of typical eating habits. In fact, they are so well informed that they could probably tell you when you will be hungry even before your body tells you.

What the advertising executives are counting on is something called *conditioned response*. Conditioned response is they way dog trainers teach their subjects how to behave, and, as tough as this may sound, you are being trained to behave a certain way every time you are exposed to the stimulus. In this case, the stimulus is hunger, and your response is to head toward a food source.

Understand that, although you may not follow through on your urge to jump in your car in search of that steak sandwich the moment you see the commercial, you *will* be more inclined to look for that sandwich restaurant the next time you experience hunger pangs when you are out and about.

The next time you see a commercial like this take note of the time, then immediately check whether you are a little hungry at the time the advertisement is being shown. Now that you are aware of this trade secret, you will most likely notice how often these companies attempt to program you to behave in certain ways.

The most outrageous thing about this type of marketing is that corporations are attempting to manipulate our responses in an effort to profit from us, without any regard for our health and well-being. They have a responsibility to create shareholder value, while you have a responsibility for your health and wealth. The value in this chapter is recognizing the tactics in use throughout the marketplace so you can prevent yourself and your family from being victims.

It is important for you to understand that in the world of personal finance, great fortunes are created by being proactive and not reactive. In other words, the corporate world is not going to knock on your door and hand you a bunch of money just because you are a nice person who happens to care about the people around you. In fact, it's the other way around. The corporate world not only expects you to give them your money, it conditions you to do so. If you are not aware of your surroundings and you remain in reactive mode, you will continue to be a victim.

Similar to the ads that target your hunger at lunchtime are the ads that take advantage of financial difficulties to draw you in. When the stock market falls, investors take losses and feel the pain of the financial squeeze. Often, gold prices will rise when stock prices fall. During these periods, it is common to see gold dealers aggressively advertising for your gold jewels and coins. They know that your stock losses are hurting you, and they're displaying the money you could make if you sent them your gold. You have to be very careful to protect against seller's remorse: selling your family jewelry at a discount for a short-term gain.

Instead of wasting energy trying to avoid the commercials, seek them out and study them. You can defend against being manipulated when you know where the strings are being pulled. You can duplicate these strategies for your own business and improve on them in ways that will benefit those with whom you do business.

Secret #3. The Infomercial

William D. Mays began his career as a salesman on the Atlantic City boardwalk. Known to his friends as Billy, he would approach passersby with a device known as the "Washmatik." His excitement over this portable washing device attracted more people than the machine itself. As his success grew, he found that he could sell almost anything as long as he believed in the product and spoke about it with enthusiasm while showing it to his prospective clients.

At a Pittsburgh home show in 1993, Billy Mays struck up a friendship with rival salesman Max Appel, who was founder of Orange Glo International, a manufacturer of cleaning products. The company had a line of products that included OxiClean, Orange Clean, and Orange Glo, all of which were eventually sold by Billy on the Home Shopping Network. Thanks to Billy's knack for selling, these products flew off the shelves and launched his career as a pitchman for many other consumable products. His trademark presentation would always start off like this: "Hi! Billy Mays here for (*advertised product*)!" His success earned him his title as "The King of Infomercials."

You should know the secret behind a successful infomercial because recognizing it will save you money as you resist the temptation to buy products you may not need. However, the secret can also work in your favor when you apply it to products of your own that others will want. These are the four parts of a successful infomercial:

1. Display the product with enthusiasm.
2. Make the offer even better by adding more value.
3. Show buyers what this value package would cost in the "real world."
4. Cut the price in half to make it irresistible to buyers while keeping it in a price range that won't hurt anyone's pocketbook.

Let's break these steps down so you can see exactly how this works. The next time you see an infomercial on the airwaves, you can go back to this list to see how the program incorporates these very same steps into the sales pitch.

1. DISPLAY THE PRODUCT WITH ENTHUSIASM.

This is where the seller identifies a need for the product. This part is likely to be as over-the-top and contrived as anything you've ever watched. Really bad actors are seen struggling with the normal ways of doing everyday chores. In seconds, almost like magic, the product turns the chore into a breeze, transforming the actor's expression into joy because of this new product.

Whether the product is a jar opener, a food container, wrinkle remover, or a belly toner, the objective here is to pique your curiosity. This is accomplished through the sales pitch, which touches on as many emotions as possible as the ad shows you how the product works.

2. MAKE THE OFFER EVEN BETTER BY ADDING MORE VALUE.

Once you are convinced that the items are a good value, the seller adds even more to the value by including other items or doubling the size of the original package. This added-value play seems almost too good to be true. While this is going on you will see satisfied customers overflowing with enthusiasm. From there, the spokesperson reviews the total package value and proceeds to the third step.

3. SHOW BUYERS WHAT THIS VALUE PACKAGE WOULD NORMALLY COST IN THE "REAL WORLD."

Showing you what this package would normally cost, if you are able to even find it in stores, is the seller's way of setting you up for the close. It doesn't really matter what price is displayed at this point because the object is simply to establish the preclose price. That's a baseline that you begin to accept as a fair value, even though it won't be the final price. If you have accepted this price as being fair, then the seller has you.

4. CUT THE PRICE IN HALF TO MAKE IT IRRESISTIBLE TO BUYERS WHILE KEEPING IT IN A PRICE RANGE THAT WON'T HURT ANYONE'S POCKETBOOK.

The seller will often cut the price in half while communicating a sense of urgency for your response. The important point to remember is that the price will be at a level that is easy to accept. In other words, most "Billy Mays"–type products are usually in the $19.95 to $29.95 price range. If the product happens to be a higher-priced item, the seller will adjust this number so it works out to be three easy payments at the acceptable price point.

Many people will buy in this $19.95 to $29.95 range because it's a price that won't hurt their pocketbooks. In fact, many infomercials add an incentive toward the end of the advertisement by saying, "And if you order right now, we will include an additional (*bonus offer*)." If you are not ready for this, you may wind up spending two to three times more than you originally bargained for simply because you are still charged up on an emotional high—a sort of buyer's feeding frenzy.

Shipping is the final piece of the pricing pie, and it can be a real kicker. It's remarkable how you can order something as insignificant as a sheet of paper and have $20 added to the cost for shipping and handling. The seller did some handling all right, but it wasn't the product that was being handled!

If you've ever flipped through the television channels at night, you've almost certainly seen the infomercials that tout the stock market as the road to riches. They march one investor after another in front of the camera to tell you about the $50,000 they made last month. In true infomercial style, they explain how anyone can do it from the comfort of his or her own home. They'll send you the training materials (shipping extra!), and you'll be on your way to wealth.

The message is the age-old get-rich-quick story. You hear about people from all walks of life who left their jobs behind to create a utopian lifestyle by following the methods offered through the infomercial. A closer examination will show you that at the bottom of each testimonial is the phrase "Results not typical." Why aren't they? If the system really worked as advertised, shouldn't the results be typical?

Secret #4. High-End Sales Reps Love It When You Shop with Your Spouse

Whenever you are looking to purchase a high-ticket item such as a home, furniture, or an insurance policy, remember that the sales reps prefer that you and your spouse be together when they are making their sales pitch. You might think the opposite would be true, but the fact is that it's harder to sell a high-ticket item to married people shopping individually than when the couple is together.

Salespeople want to close the deal as quickly as possible, and for married couples that often requires the consent of both partners. The moment you tell them you have to speak with your spouse before making a decision, they realize that the chance of making the sale has dropped considerably. The fact that you are going home to think about the purchase is actually a take-charge response. That gives you time to cool down and pull yourself away from the emotions that cause an impulse buy. Here are a few other steps you can take before making a large purchase:

- *If you are married, meet with the sales reps alone.* Not only does this help you avoid making an impulse buy, it also gives you a good excuse to leave the meeting when a salesperson tries to hard-sell you.

- *Divide-and-conquer is a strategy you can use to negotiate a good deal.* If you and your spouse have found competitive pricing somewhere else, pit one deal against the other as the sellers compete for your business.

- *Simply take a breather.* The item was there yesterday, and it will be there tomorrow. You'll hear various reasons to explain why today is the day you need to make the purchase. Rest assured that if you walk in tomorrow with cash, they won't turn down a deal.

- *Shop with an experienced friend.* This may be your first time at bat in this particular game, but you probably know someone who has been down this road before you.

- *Do your homework.* There's no excuse for shopping blind these days. You can find research, reviews, pricing, and customer comments on just about any product or service. Have your information in hand when you shop.

These strategies work as well for major financial purchases as they do for appliances and cars. The next time you refinance your home or renew your insurance, run through these steps. For example, a great way to do some homework online is to look at your local mortgage rates through Bankrate.com. This service lists the various lenders, along with their rates and loan terms, so that you can compare loans in a single location. Once you've narrowed down your choices for your mortgage, you should know that your broker is required to give you a good faith estimate (GFE) of your closing fees and settlement charges. This is your document for comparing loans. Don't rely on the word of your broker. He or she might not be intentionally misleading you, but there are too many details to rely on a verbal description of the loan. The website for the U.S. Department of Housing and Urban Development (HUD, www.hud.gov) has a GFE comparison chart that is similar to the following:

	LOAN 1	LOAN 2	LOAN 3	LOAN 4	LOAN 5
LENDER					
LOAN AMOUNT					
LOAN TERM					
INTEREST RATE					
MONTHLY PAYMENT					
RATE LOCK PERIOD					
CAN RATE RISE?					
CAN BALANCE RISE?					
CAN MONTHLY PAYMENT RISE?					
PREPAYMENT PENALTY?					
BALLOON PAYMENT?					
TOTAL ESTIMATED SETTLEMENT CHARGES					

Unwritten Rules

It would be hard to imagine a new trader stepping onto the floor of the stock exchange without understanding the formal rules and the unwritten rules. The written rules are easy; they're the guidelines that govern the activity on the trading floor. The unwritten rules are the tough ones. You need someone to show you the ropes in advance, or you'll learn the hard way—and the latter is much more expensive.

Your marketplace is much the same. The unwritten rules that dictate the way business operates are not illegal or even necessarily unethical. They exist and drive consumer behavior nonetheless. Handle your money like a financial professional by knowing all the rules of the game, written and unwritten!

Chapter 10

Invest without Fear

Investing without fear requires that you maintain a healthy respect for the markets. The absence of fear as well as respect exists only in a novice investor. It is only a matter of time before one or both emotions are painfully reinstated.

Before you can learn how to invest without fear, it's important for you to understand what causes fear in the first place. Fear is a state of mind that causes us to believe harm will result from being exposed to things we perceive as dangerous. In other words, fear is a natural reaction to potential danger and is something science looks upon as a survival instinct. But when we allow fear to take over in other areas of our lives, it can be as destructive as the things we dread most, especially when it pertains to our finances.

We need to make the distinction between true fear and the idea of fear in the popular culture. In the context of this discussion, we're talking about an undercurrent of fear that is constantly present. This is quite different from responding with momentary fright. Some humorous programs, such as *Just for Laughs,* have been big hits on television and online because they caught people in the act of being scared. If we're honest, many of us would have to admit to the fun of catching someone in that vulnerable moment when we burst into sight and scare the living daylights out of her. That's fun, not fear.

The point is, when you allow yourself to fall into a situation where you have become oblivious to your surroundings, you open yourself up to fear. Preparing yourself for the unexpected helps remove any fear and leaves you in a state of readiness, which is much better than allowing yourself to remain in a fearful state.

Fear Can Affect People and Nations

There have been times when people were so overtaken by fear that, at least for a short period, it paralyzed nations. The attacks on the World Trade Center and the Pentagon on September 11, 2001, for example, generated a new level of fear in the U.S. population. The use of commercial aircraft to launch terrorist attacks was so unexpected that it immediately created enough fear to cause people to avoid flying altogether—a fear that lasts to this day for some people. Governments have since learned how to better prepare for such situations, and as a result of this preparedness, much of the fear has been removed.

The magnitude of the market turmoil of 2008 and 2009 was due in large part to an epidemic of fear. Many very good companies watched as their stock prices plummeted. Although many of these companies were on solid footing, investors were spooked by the economic reports and anecdotal stories of sporadic business failures. When fear grips investors, the markets suffer as a whole.

Identifying the Fear

Most fears are easily overcome once a person has an understanding of the perceived threat. Identifying the threat is the first step in overcoming the fear and taking charge of your emotions.

There are more than five hundred documented phobias, some of which are the fear of spiders (arachnophobia), the fear of snakes (ophidiophobia), and the terror that results from being in confined spaces (claustrophobia). While we were doing our research, we found other interesting phobias such as the understandable fear of atomic explosions (atomosophobia) and the fear of air, especially drafts (aerophobia). Apparently, some folks have a fear of bald people (peladophobia).One of the most common fears is that of public speaking (glossophobia). It's been said that the majority of people would rather attend their own funeral than speak at someone else's.

What surprised us the most is that we had a difficult time finding a term that best described the fear of losing money. We know this fear exists because the fear of losing money, together with another force called greed, are among the most powerful economic forces in the world. These forces are what drive prices up and down in the stock market, and they are even strong enough to trigger global recessions. We couldn't ignore this, so we decided to create our own term to describe the fear of losing money: *fiscalcatastrophobia.*

Fiscalcatastrophobia

Fear and money mix about as well as fire and gasoline. They can be brought together, but the results are explosive. Because we have seen so many people destroy themselves as a result of this fear, we felt compelled to discuss it in this book. There are two assumptions we can make based on our experience:

1. Greed leads to fiscalcatastrophobia.
2. Financial education, grounded in sound risk management principles, works to eliminate fiscalcatastrophobia.

Fear always surfaces when you are investing in something about which you know very little. Furthermore, your level of fear increases in direct proportion to the size of your investment. Real estate, artwork, new businesses, stocks in unfamiliar sectors, and investments in countries that are politically unstable can create fear if you have little experience with them.

Greed leads many investors to wade into unknown waters. They hear that a fortune can be made in real estate, so they begin to buy foreclosure properties. A late-night infomercial touts opportunities in gold, so they start trading commodities. Greed causes them to jump into unfamiliar investments so they don't miss out on the profits that they perceive everyone else to be reaping. Although greed draws them in, fear of the unknown soon takes over and paralyzes their actions. Together, the twin forces of greed and fear sap away any semblance of control that these investors might have had. They are no longer in charge of their money.

Greed Causes Fear

Investing with the intention of selling later for a profit is simply an example of being a good steward. Whether we are investing our time or our money, we expect to get paid a reasonable and fair return for our investments. This is not greed. The desire to buy something now as an investment with a plan to sell it later for a profit is a goal shared by all good stewards. If it turns out that our investments are not allowing us to accomplish this, then we simply adjust our position by looking for other investments that will allow us to reach our financial goals.

Greed is different. Greed is motivating someone who is looking to buy now because any delay would result in missed profits. The greed is magnified when others are seen to be collecting those profits. Greed is the little voice in the back of your mind that whispers suggestions that might be better suited to gambling in a casino. Roll the dice and hope for the best. Greed steers you toward the fast money, the quick buck. It's what appeals most to unsuspecting investors who know little about the way things should really work.

Greedy people are suckers for the snake oil salesmen who promise to get you something for nothing. Greed does not discriminate. It takes down the multibillion-dollar hedge fund manager as quickly as it takes down Grandma and her retirement account.

Removing Greed

One of the first things you can do for yourself is create a plan. Emotions are susceptible to greed, and a plan helps you keep your emotions in check. When you understand the market you're investing in and you have goals to reach for, greed and fear diminish. Your goals include getting a fair and reasonable return over a longer period of time. This is the exact opposite of what greedy investors do—they look for a quick turnover in typically high-risk transactions.

When we talk about understanding your market, we're not just referring to the trading and investing side. It is profitable to know what drives values within that market. For example, the Atlantic hurricane season officially begins on June 1 each year and lasts until November 30. Storms develop off the coast of Africa that eventually head west over the Atlantic Ocean toward the Caribbean Islands and the southeastern shores of the United States. These storms can have a profound influence on some types of investments, even to the point of allowing you to profit.

Think about the residual effects in the market after a hurricane. Home builders, lumber companies, battery companies, and bottled water companies all see business increases following a major storm. So how does this allow you to profit? You identify the money flow and follow the money. Insurance companies are likely to post losses after a hurricane, while building supply stores generally post profits. We are not talking about making money from the misfortune of others; we are talking about money flow and how you can position yourself in the direction of the money as an investor.

The following list provides some more ideas for tracking events and circumstances that have major influences on markets. Of course, feel free to do your own study and find others that might work better for you. Use the following seasonal list to get the wheels turning:

- Winter features blizzards, snow shovels, holiday travel, and a need for heating oil. Consider investing in companies like utilities, airlines, retailers, and shipping services.

- Spring brings weddings, flowers, and tax season, as well as cleanup from the winter mess. Profit from this season by investing in home improvement, landscaping, accounting and legal firms, and clothing.

- Summer is the time for vacations, travel, barbecues, and family outings. Money flows into vacation rentals, airlines, grocers, and oil and energy companies.

- Autumn means money moves into back-to-school items, children's clothing, books, and transportation companies. The holidays stimulate sales of chocolate, turkeys, hams, and baked items.

Know Your Limits

Did you know that the Securities and Exchange Commission (SEC) requires brokerage firms to identify their clients' comfort zones according to *suitability rules*? These rules are imposed by self-regulatory organizations like the New York Stock Exchange and the National Association of Securities Dealers (NASD). They have been put into place to protect investors from brokers who might sell them investments that fall outside of their investment objectives and risk tolerance levels.

According to SEC Rule 17a-3(17), brokerage firms are required to keep a record for each investor that includes the investor's name, address, phone number, and tax ID number. In addition to this, the broker is required to ask for information about the person's occupation, date of birth, annual income, net worth, and investment objectives. Brokers are also required to update this suitability profile every three years. The reason brokers collect and maintain this suitability profile is to ensure that they don't purchase investments that are inappropriate for you. If you're nearing retirement, it would be wrong to buy a mutual fund with a load. A load is a declining fee that disappears after about five to ten years. But if you need your money before the load expires, you'll pay more than you should. That fails the suitability test. If this is so important that the regulators have established hard rules for identifying an investor's objectives, then why wouldn't you do this in managing your own personal finances?

The following is a checklist that you can keep in your records that will not only help you stay the course but also help you stay within your comfort zone. Remember that when you are comfortable with your investments you are less likely to fear the unknown.

- Know your own suitability profile. Make sure you are comfortable with your investment strategies. Use the Chapter 10 checklist in the workbook to ensure that you choose investments that are appropriate for your risk tolerance.

- Are you risking more than you can afford to lose? If so, then you must correct this by either risking less in the investment or boosting your capital. Your risk in an investment should always be proportional to your capital. High-net-worth investors can risk more money because it represents a smaller percentage of their assets. We recommend limiting your loss to 1 percent of your account value if your investment is for less than one year. If your investment is for longer than one year, you should limit your loss to 2 to 3 percent of your account value.

- Understand that it is better to win a lot of smaller battles than to put everything you have into winning a big battle. You may have heard that the way to win a baseball game is with many singles and doubles rather than home runs. Why? Because the likelihood of a home run is small, while the singles and doubles add up over time. Don't try to get rich with a hot stock tip. Stay disciplined and make a little at a time with sound investments.

- Keep most of your money in high-quality investments. People with very little to invest tend to try to gamble their way to riches. It's the lottery ticket mentality. Avoid this trap by staying away from speculators.

- Outline a procedure that allows you to make decisions in an unemotional way. Emotions do you no good when you are trying to carry out a financial plan.

If you discover, after you have gone through the Chapter 10 checklist in the workbook, that you have a low risk tolerance, our advice is that you stay away from the stock market and look at investments with a risk level that you can tolerate. The goal of this chapter is to help you invest without fear. Franklin D. Roosevelt said it best in his 1933 inauguration speech: " . . . the only thing we have to fear is fear itself."

Fear can paralyze you if you let it. It gets in the way of realizing your financial goals, and it causes you to make poor financial decisions. Conquer your fear of the unknown through learning. Begin to invest without fear, and take charge of your money!

PART FOUR

The Purpose

Chapter 11
The Threat of Complacency

The three steps in self-defense are awareness, avoidance, and attack. What is true for personal defense is true for financial defense: You must be aware of your environment and avoid the dangers.

There is no question that we are living in troubled times. We can clearly see economic uncertainty, political unrest, and global tensions between world powers. Unfortunately, our long stretch of prosperity has left many of us complacent and unwilling or unable to take action when necessary. It's as though a whole nation has been paralyzed by the freedom and relative wealth we've enjoyed for decades. Out of complacency we have allowed CEOs to steal from their shareholders, in the form of golden parachutes and stock options. We have also watched as many of these CEOs and accountants conspired to channel stockholder value into their own pockets by falsifying reports, misleading analysts, and presenting disingenuous answers to direct questions. Then we sit back and watch the news headlines as these same CEOs bankrupt the very corporations that support our nation's economy. Our call to you today is a wake-up call.

Are You Ready for Action?

Are you ready to take action yet? Have you felt enough pain after watching the corruption at the corporate and political levels? Are you going to just sit back and hope everything will be okay in your life, or are you going to stand up and take charge of your financial and personal life?

> ● CHATTER BOX **AJ**
>
> Going back to my military days, I can recall the drills we conducted to prepare for emergency situations. When a naval vessel falls under attack, a call goes out to everyone in the battle group: "General Quarters, General Quarters, all hands man your battle stations." When the alarm was sounded, everyone knew exactly where to go and what role they would be playing to secure the ship and prepare for an attack.

What we are going to give you now is your own General Quarters exercise, so you can prepare for any financial attack should one come about. Knowing you have a plan that can help protect you and your family will bring you peace of mind. These simple steps will enhance your state of readiness and allow you to act quickly to ward off any short-term threats that could jeopardize your financial condition.

- GET INVOLVED IN LOCAL ISSUES.
  Remember that the United States is a republic. You have a voice in preparing for and protecting against financial disasters, natural or manmade. Hold your elected officials accountable, and stick together as a community. You will be amazed at the opportunities that arise when like-minded individuals get together. Not only are you helping to keep the lines of commu-

nication open, but it is fun, and you will make many friends as a result.

- **REVIEW YOUR FINANCIAL GOALS AND YOUR PLAN REGULARLY.**
Make sure you go over this plan on a regular basis and include members of your family so they are aware of your plans. This is similar to conducting a fire drill. Everyone knows where to meet, and everyone is aware of their escape route so they don't have to think about it in the heat of the moment. Rehearsing it enables a speedy execution.

- **ELIMINATE DEBT AS QUICKLY AS POSSIBLE.**
Debt will keep you from responding to changes in your finances or the economy in general. You will not be able to capture opportunities that arise during periods of economic transition and turmoil. If your debt load is heavy as a result of poor budget discipline, you will not have any leeway to add short-term debt to meet your needs if required in an emergency. Companies have credit lines to carry them through times of turmoil. Your credit line is gone if you've already used it by overspending now.

- **CREATE AN EMERGENCY CASH FUND.**
Even if you set aside only a few dollars each week, you should have your hands on a small amount of cash. An emergency might be limited to your family or it might be broader, reaching your community or beyond. Cash gives you the flexibility to make necessary short-term purchases. Don't hoard cash instead of investing; just keep enough accessible for items such as food and gas.

- **BE ON THE HUNT FOR OPPORTUNITIES.**
Each week make a list of ideas that you think would allow you to profit. For instance, if you think the price of oil is going to go up and possibly reach record high levels, what industries do you think would do well? Wind power, solar power, nuclear

power, and other alternative energy sources are places you should consider as an investor. What else can you do to realize a profit in addition to simply investing money in such companies? Do you know enough about this industry to become a consultant? Opportunities are not going to just show up on your doorstep. Stay active and alert; be on the hunt for them.

This Is the Moment!

This chapter is not intended to leave you feeling warm and fuzzy. Battle lines are being drawn, with the forces of Wall Street, Washington politics, and international powers arrayed on one side. On the other side are the men, women, and children of Main Street. You are the fuel that drives the world's greatest economy. Your task now is to penetrate those battle lines, and get involved in new and exciting ways.

Begin by taking charge of your own money. Then embark on your mission to help your friends and family do the same. Next, hold Wall Street and Washington accountable. Thinking about the possibilities can be exciting, but you must first realize that complacency is a real threat—and don't fall prey to it. Instead, use your time to get your own financial house in order, and then reach out to other people and institutions in your area to help them do the same.

Chapter 12

What Is Your Purpose?

We don't need more financial Don Quixotes, who attack the insignificant issues. The world cries for men and women of focus, drive, and determination, who will take charge of their money and help others do the same along the way.

Do you know this person? He rises without hitting the snooze button. He does his job without complaining while at the same time working longer and harder than anyone around him. He delivers on time and works for something that's deeper than the surface.

This person has his own set of standards and expectations, far beyond what the average person would even consider. You know him when he walks into a room. You might describe him as confident, focused, steady on his feet, and unshakeable. He is in complete control of his mind, and he appears fearless. You can feel his presence and realize that this is a man whom you would follow. What we have just described to you is a person with a purpose.

Those who have a purpose will tell you that they don't need anyone else's permission, endorsement, or acknowledgment to complete their tasks. They know exactly who they are and what they need to accomplish. They are driven individuals who are happy with their lives. There is a certain freedom in having a purpose in life because it provides a confidence that surpasses one's abilities. That's not to say that a purpose causes you to lose perspective about what you can accomplish. Rather, you can accomplish more as your skills and abilities follow your drive toward your purpose. Those with a sense of purpose welcome challenges because they know that challenges make them stronger.

Thomas Paine said:

> *The harder the conflict, the more glorious the triumph. What we obtain too cheap, we esteem too lightly; 'tis dearness only that gives everything its value. I love the man that can smile in trouble, that can gather strength from distress and grow brave by reflection. 'Tis the business of little minds to shrink; but he whose heart is firm, and whose conscience approves his conduct, will pursue his principles unto death.*

Purpose-driven people pay the price of success gladly. They are warriors who are willing to fight for their purpose, and they draw their strength from within.

Who Are You?

We have met many thousands of people around the world and have had the opportunity to reach millions of others through television and radio. Over the years, we have found that many of those who come up to us as we step off the stage at our seminars are people who have already found their purpose. We'd like to share Tony Macken's and Kathleen Farrelly's story because it is so compelling.

● CHATTER BOX **AJ**

Tony and Kathleen, whom we first met at a Tony Robbins Wealth Mastery seminar where A.J. was speaking, were avid note takers as they listened to the experts talk about ways to build a business and invest in the stock market. There was so much information coming at them in such a short period of time that they felt as though their heads couldn't contain all of it. Toward the end of the four-day event, they realized that there was more to making money than just accumulating personal wealth and profiting in the stock market. This was when they hatched their plan.

They wanted to make a difference in the world that reached beyond wealth. They knew they had enough information to make a profit for themselves, but Tony and Kathleen realized that they had a new purpose in life. They later told us that once they had made their decision to make a difference, they knew that success depended on their total commitment to their cause. As they said, "If we are going to do this, then we a going to have to go big with it." And big it was!

They immediately started a nonprofit foundation called Giving While Living. They had a focused goal to raise money for those in need. Being the world travelers that they were, they decided to take a motorcycle ride. Their idea: to ride from Capetown, South Africa, to Cork, Ireland, with a goal of raising $40,000 for a deserving cause.

We are talking about a distance of 19,545 kilometers (12,144 miles), which would require them to travel through some of the most dangerous regions of the world. To put this into perspective, the average American travels 12,000 miles per year in a car, driving on well-paved roads that are relatively safe. Tony and Kathleen would have to travel this same distance, but on two wheels and on roads that were barely cleared, let alone paved.

They so strongly believed in their purpose that they were willing to risk their lives for this cause. The risks were enormous, but they were convinced the rewards would far outweigh them. Not only did they have to watch out for road bandits and thieves, but at times they were totally exposed in the bush to wild animals that saw them as prey. There were occasions when their equipment broke down, when

Chatterbox continues

they were without fuel, and when they had trouble finding the right currency to pay for food. On top of that, they were exposed to potentially fatal diseases. In short, they battled forces and elements with the passion of those possessed by a purpose.

What they ultimately accomplished is something you might see only in the movies or in an action novel. They achieved their goal of raising $40,000, but the interesting twist in this story is that in finding their own purpose, Tony and Kathleen crossed paths with someone else who was driven by a strong sense of purpose.

Billy Riordan had fallen in love with the small Central African village of Cape McClear, and the people who lived in this place that he described in an e-mail to his mother, Mags Riordan, as "paradise." Ironically, less than forty-eight hours after sending this message, Billy drowned in Lake Malawi at the age of twenty-five.

In February 2000, one year after his death, Mags traveled to Cape McClear to deliver a memorial stone to the lake in honor of her son's life. She ended up spending three months there, getting to know the villagers and their way of life, just as Billy had. The poverty in the village was so severe that she returned to the village on five separate occasions over a two-and-a-half-year period in an effort to help them. Ultimately, she went back to teach in the primary school.

The challenges that Tony and Kathleen overcame on their journey ultimately led them to Mags Riordan, whose own challenge was losing her only son, Billy. But thanks to Mags, Billy's death was not in vain: She founded Billy's Walawi Project, Inc., and Tony and Kathleen donated the money they had raised to this organization. As a result of their efforts to make a positive difference in the world, children in this area are now receiving an education, and a medical clinic that bears Billy's name has been built there. This story illustrates in a profound way Thomas Paine's notion of triumphing through overcoming conflict.

Start Small, Dream Big

Doug Rodante is a pilot and a friend of The Market Guys. Doug was living in Florida on August 24, 2005, when Hurricane Katrina hit the east coast of the state as a moderate Category 1 hurricane. By the time Katrina departed the west coast of Florida, it had become a reorganized Category 5 monster. On August 29, Katrina hit New Orleans like an atomic bomb, leaving destruction in her wake. Katrina became one of the deadliest storms ever to hit the United States.

Doug knew he couldn't just sit there and do nothing, so he quickly organized a relief team that included Joe Hurston, president of Air Mobile Ministries, and they took to the skies to deliver water purification equipment to the rescue teams in New Orleans.

Shortly afterward, Doug found himself knee-deep in some of the most contaminated water imaginable, doing his best to get fresh water to the desperate residents of New Orleans. There was real danger in trying to maneuver through the debris. The last thing anyone wanted to do was step on a nail or get cut on the jagged metal and broken glass that was all around them. A laceration in these waters could mean contracting a potentially deadly disease like dysentery, cholera, or hepatitis. The rescue process was slow, but they eventually got the job done.

As the seasons passed, it seemed as though there was one disaster after another, and, throughout, Doug knew what he had to do. Eventually, he realized that he had more to offer the world than water purification machines. He turned his attention from water to oil.

If the most polluted water imaginable could be purified to the point where it could be ingested, then what was to stop him from purifying cooking oil so that it could be used as fuel? Doug had found his purpose.

Once again, he surrounded himself with a team of engineers, scientists, pilots, and energy consultants. On October 2, 2007, Doug's new company, Greenflight International, successfully completed the world's first jet aircraft flight powered by 100 percent biofuel. On November 1, 2008, the team made history again when they completed the first transcontinental jet flight powered entirely by biofuel. Isn't it amazing what can happen when you have a dream and a purpose?

What's Your Dream?

We freely and publicly acknowledge that our purpose is to help you find direction, not only in the financial world but in your personal world as well. Somewhere right now you might be reading these words and your mind is yelling, "Hey! These guys are talking to me! I get it!"

That means we have somehow managed to connect with you, and we don't believe a coincidence brought us together. Perhaps the timing of this book couldn't be better for this stage of your life. You might be gathering information for a friend or loved one to help them out of a bad situation. Whatever the case, if you want to get the most out of this book, you must make a commitment to yourself right now that you *are* going to take charge of your money! But don't let it stop there.

Use your money to meet the needs of yourself and your family, but also plan to use some of this money to make a contribution to the world. You don't have to start off with a grand plan like Tony and Kathleen did when they traveled thousands of miles for their cause. Nor are we asking you to risk your life in the process. Take some time and find a quiet place. Block out all immediate distractions, and imagine things you would like to do with your life that would make a positive difference in the world. If you are a spiritual person, then feel free to pray for guidance. You can start small and build on your plan. Little by little, you will notice that you are making a difference. When this happens, you will know that you are on the right path and you will have changed the world for the better.

Without question, life will challenge you at times. The challenge may be financial or personal, but whatever it is, the strength you will need to overcome it arises from a place deep inside you. Your strength may lie in your confidence, in your faith, or perhaps in both. You can find solace from those around you who believe in your purpose because first they learned to believe in you.

If you have read everything in this book to this point and arrived at this paragraph, we congratulate you! You have become empowered in a way that you may have never realized until now. You have followed the guidance we offered here, and you have the tools to change your life. As John Donne said, "No man is an island, entire of itself." When your life changes, change will flow in every direction around you. Your children, parents, brothers, sisters, friends, and coworkers may be inspired by what you commit to today.

Take charge of your money now! Change your life! Change your world!

PART FIVE

The Unexpected

Chapter 13

Taking Charge of the Unexpected

The prudent captain prepares his vessel for rough seas in the calm of the harbor. You can't know when or where the rough seas will hit your finances, but preparation now will help you navigate safely later.

We're not telling you anything new. Life comes with surprises. In spite of your best preparation, sometimes events turn in a way that you could neither predict nor control. In other cases, you knew the event was coming, but you didn't quite appreciate the magnitude of the impact of that event. Such is the case with a new family. Of course, you're excited about the prospect of the baby joining your family. And plenty of your friends and family have been down that road before (your parents, at least). But you're still not entirely prepared for the changes that you'll experience in many areas of your life: diapers, sleep schedules, and finances.

Nationwide ran a series of funny commercials about how fast life comes at you. Sometimes it is the unexpected; sometimes it is the expected arriving faster than you had thought it would. In one ad, a butterfly lands on a car, triggering the alarm and setting into motion a series of events that culminates in a boat crashing through the roof of a house. Clearly, the homeowner wasn't prepared for that eventuality. Humor aside, what will you do if the improbable becomes reality? Will you allow your finances to spiral out of control, or will you be ready to take charge of your money in the middle of the storm?

This chapter discusses some of the more common situations that you might face. For each situation, we discuss five major financial considerations to help you take charge of your money. These lists are not meant to be comprehensive; there are likely other issues that would apply to your unique situation. Nor are the lists provided in complete detail. We expect that you'll dig deeper into the topics that apply to you. This is especially true with issues that have legal ramifications such as bankruptcy, divorce, and identity theft. Please use this chapter as a guide, not a substitute for proper legal or professional counsel. Think of this chapter as your road map. If you want to find a specific office in a high-rise, you first need a road map to get you to the city where the office is located. A second, much more detailed, map will take you to the right building, floor, and office. This chapter takes you to the city.

The goal in this chapter is to show you how to take the Pareto approach. The Pareto principle is the old 80/20 rule—80 percent of the results are achieved by focusing on 20 percent of the problems. A pitfall of finding yourself in one of the situations we'll discuss is that you can quickly become overwhelmed by circumstances. You are not a failure if you don't cover all five of the topics we address. Start with one, and take charge of that small issue. Then move to the next topic on the list. Steady steps toward your goal will spell the difference between winning and losing. Don't fix the entire problem at once. That's not a reasonable goal. If you can attack the lion's share of the challenges you'll face—one step at a time—then you'll be in a position to take charge!

The following list (in alphabetical order) contains the special circumstances we'll cover:

- Bankruptcy
- Catastrophic expense
- College students

- Divorce
- Foreclosure
- Identity theft
- Job loss
- Marriage
- Retirement
- Starting a family
- Windfalls—lottery, bonuses

Many of the issues we cover apply to more than one special circumstance. For example, the discussion on rebuilding personal credit after a divorce is equally important to a college student who needs to build a credit history for the first time. Take the time to review all of the topics in this chapter, and we're sure you will find ideas to help you take charge of your money. One of the hallmarks of a good professional on Wall Street is that he or she learns lessons from someone else's mistakes if possible. Wouldn't it be great if you could apply some of these ideas without the hard life experiences?

Bankruptcy

1. Chapter 7 versus Chapter 13

One of the main purposes of filing for bankruptcy is to give you the ability to start fresh. In playground language, it's a do-over. Filing for bankruptcy is not to be taken lightly. This is a big deal for you financially and should be looked at as one of the last resorts, not the first. However, if you are so buried in debt that there is no light at the end of the tunnel, this course of action might be best. Whether your reason for considering bankruptcy is your lack of fiscal responsibility or that you have been a victim of extraordinary circumstances such as overwhelming medical bills, you have to decide which bankruptcy path to take.

Chapter 7 is the bankruptcy filing that basically liquidates your assets and wipes the slate clean. Under Chapter 7, your eligible debts are discharged and your nonexempt assets are turned into cash and distributed to your creditors. Some assets, such as retirement accounts, are exempt from bankruptcy liquidation. You should be aware that Chapter 7 doesn't get rid of all your debt obligations. Some debts that remain after bankruptcy include taxes, student loans, and child support.

Chapter 13 is also known as *reorganization bankruptcy*. Rather than turning your possessions into cash and discharging your debt, you are simply appealing for time and help in getting your finances in order. Typically, a Chapter 13 bankruptcy filing gives you three to five years to restructure your debts and pay off your obligations. Chapter 13 is also a better choice if you have valuable nonexempt assets. Remember, with a Chapter 7 filing, your valuables are sold off to pay your debts. If you have many valuable possessions that you would lose with a Chapter 7 filing, it may be better to file under Chapter 13, which lets you work out a plan to eliminate your debt without requiring that you forfeit your possessions.

2. Credit Counselors

One of the requirements in bankruptcy filing is that you take an approved credit counseling course. Many people who get to the point where they're considering bankruptcy start to look for credit counselors anyway. With the rise in consumer debt over the past decade, hundreds of credit counseling agencies have sprung up.

A credit counselor can help you in a number of ways, including:

- Prebankruptcy counseling
- Managing family budgets
- Establishing credit
- Setting financial goals
- Creating a debt management plan (DMP)

As with any fast-moving industry, there are good people and there are swindlers. This is not the time to open yourself up to a swindler. Start off by telling yourself that you will find the counselor, rather than vice versa. Don't think it a divine intervention if, at the very moment you decide to find a credit counselor, you get an unsolicited e-mail from a counseling service. That's not divine; that's spam. Look up one of the nonprofit consumer advocacy groups that specialize in credit counseling and pick from their member list. The U.S. Trustee Program (www.usdoj.gov/ust) also provides a list of approved credit counseling agencies, organized by state.

3. Protect Your Retirement

As a broad rule, retirement accounts have been excluded from liquidation in a bankruptcy filing. The specific laws have varied over the years regarding the types of accounts that are exempt, the limits (if any) that are placed on the exemption, and the way distributions from retirement accounts are treated. The key point to recognize here is that retirement accounts are handled differently than your general savings and investment accounts.

Additionally, the Bankruptcy Abuse Prevention and Consumer Protection Act of 2005 (BAPCPA) includes protection for some education savings accounts. BAPCPA protects contributions made more than two years before the bankruptcy filing to education savings accounts for your child or grandchild. For more information about BAPCPA, go to www.usdoj.gov/ust/eo/bapcpa/index.htm.

Why is this important to you now? Because bankruptcy is not intended to eliminate any chance of recovery for you. You need to know that there are certain areas where you can save money, and those areas will be protected even if the rest of the house falls. It's a bit like a storm shelter. You might suffer the loss of the big house, but you'll still have something in which to take shelter and to build upon. For that reason, you should continue to be diligent in funding your retirement and education accounts while the weather is clear.

4. Rebuilding Credit

One of your goals after deciding to file bankruptcy is to make sure that your new financial house is built on a solid foundation.

Bankruptcy teaches you some tough life lessons, so don't let them go to waste. Figure out what you need to do differently when you make your new start, and be disciplined. Don't throw in the towel after bankruptcy, figuring that you blew it and there's no reason to rebuild.

● CHATTER BOX **Rick**

Most financial professionals have either taken a significant loss or been close to someone who has. The reason is simple: You don't truly develop a deep respect for risk management until you taste the fruit of poor risk management. When I was a novice trader, I relied on a software program that I had written to generate trades. I fed the market data into the program, and it told me when to buy and sell. The fatal flaw there was that I didn't have a contingency plan for when the program went awry. I assumed that the effort I put into creating the program would ensure that my trades were correct.

This all worked well until the day it didn't work! That night, I went home after having lost over $50,000 in a single day. Fortunately for me, the markets reversed course overnight, and I was able to close my trades within the first hour at a small profit.

AJ's story is a little different. He, too, suffered losses in the silver market, but his markets didn't reverse course overnight. Instead, he watched as the markets closed for several days due to a lack of buyers. Quite simply, he wanted to sell his silver, but, there wasn't a buyer to be found! It took AJ several years to rebuild what he had lost in several days.

In order to rebuild your credit, you need to use credit. This may seem counterintuitive after filing for bankruptcy. Why use credit when that got you into trouble the first time? It wasn't the *use* of credit that got you into trouble; it was the *misuse* of credit. We're talking about getting credit and using it in a very deliberate and re-sponsible manner. Take charge of your credit, and you'll be well on your way to taking charge of your money.

Start by paying close attention to your credit report. You have to know the score before you can make improvements; otherwise, you're shooting in the dark. Get your credit report and review your strengths and weaknesses. The major credit reporting companies (Equifax.com, Experian.com, and Transunion.com) will help you evaluate the areas where you can make improvements. Remind yourself that this is a process that builds over time. You don't jump right back in and fix your credit tomorrow. You build it with pa-tience, discipline, and determination. Follow these action steps to stay on track with rebuilding your credit:

- Pay on time. Use automatic payments to assist you.
- Don't use your entire credit line. Try to keep your credit card balances to less than 50 percent of your available credit.
- Use a secured credit card if you don't have a standard credit card.
- Correct any errors on your credit report by contacting the reporting agency in writing.
- Get small retail store cards and pay the balance in full or make steady payments.
- Space your new credit accounts at least two months apart. Having too many account applications in a short period drops your credit score.
- Don't limit your credit to cards only. A car loan or student loan, for example, builds your credit with more than just revolving debt.

5. Start Your Financial Diet

Filing for bankruptcy without making any changes to your money habits is like stopping at a burger joint for a double-decker with fries on your way home from bypass surgery. You have to shift gears now, or you'll be right back here all over again. Maybe you were responsible with your money, and your bankruptcy was the result of an unfortunate circumstance. In that case, you may just need to do some temporary belt tightening beyond the way you normally operate. It's true that bankruptcy hits some people who have managed their finances well throughout their life.

On the other hand, your bankruptcy might have been the result of carefree spending and a complete lack of control over your money. If you fall into that category, then this is the time to start your crash diet. It has been said that insanity is doing the same things and expecting different results. If you don't want to go bankrupt again, you need to identify the habits that brought you to this point. Here are some ideas for how you can jump-start your new financial diet:

- *You don't need the latest and greatest.* Make do with your old mobile phone instead of the newest model.

- *Skip the treats.* Five-dollar coffees may not seem like much at the time, but if you're not meeting your debts, you don't need them.

- *Downgrade.* You can afford a lot of repair bills on an older car for the same amount of money you're shelling out for a new car payment.

- *Downsize.* We used to watch TV on screens that were smaller than a billboard. And we did it in houses that didn't look like small hotels.

- *Count to ten.* Impulse buying is a dangerous habit. If you think you need to buy something, stop and reconsider the purchase tomorrow or next week. Taking a breather helps you overcome impulse buying.

- *True friends can't be bought.* If you're the life of the party because you pick up the tab, find another party.

- *Give yourself an allowance.* Make a budget and stick to it. If you need more tomorrow, make do with less today. Follow the Family Budget guidelines in the workbook, and pay particular attention to the spending chapter.

Catastrophic Expenses

1. Circle the Wagons

Catastrophic expenses, by definition, are those financial events that hit you hard and suddenly. They can take the form of a natural disaster, a fire, an accident, an illness, or a lawsuit. In whatever form they occur, the result to your pocketbook is the same. You find yourself in a position that you could hardly plan for, and it is has become the elephant in the room. No matter how much you might try, you can't ignore or deny it.

Your first reaction when hit with a catastrophic expense is to go into survival mode. You need to circle the wagons. Just as in the frontier days, circling the wagons means you have to protect yourself and your family from further attack. You have to gather your resources, identify your position, and make sure you don't suffer further loss.

From a financial perspective, this is accomplished by making sure you know exactly where you are with your money. If you haven't been in the habit of reconciling credit card statements, bank accounts, and checkbooks, now is the time to start. Second, you need to know exactly where your money is being spent. You will begin plugging any and all holes in your cash flow. Look for things like automatic monthly deductions for services such as music downloads and book clubs. Turn those off now. Then walk through your expenses and find out where you can cut to the bone. Eating out? Nope. Car washes? Finished. Lawn maintenance? Next year. If you go into crisis mode immediately and circle the wagons, you have a very good chance of minimizing the impact and duration of the catastrophic expense so that you can resume normal life.

2. Beware of Fire Sales

You may be tempted to abandon ship if a catastrophic expense is what causes stormy seas for your money. Some may tell you to sell your assets and generate as much cash as possible. There are times when that might be a good idea, but we want you to make that decision with your head rather than your heart. A fire sale occurs when you sell a dollar for a dime because you desperately need the dime. What we're saying to you is this: Make sure you can't get the dime any other way before you start selling your dollars.

Some property is fairly easy to sell, especially on the online auction sites. With the right market, you might get a decent price, and it makes sense for you to sell the asset and use the cash to help you recover from the catastrophic expense. Other property may not fetch the best price, but it is something that you can certainly live without. If you can collect enough to make the sale worthwhile and eliminate some of the expenses, then go ahead and put it up for sale.

What you shouldn't do is make a decision you'll regret long after the storm has passed. Some people in such a circumstance look at family heirlooms or jewelry as quick sources of cash. Your grandmother's gold bracelet might be very easy to liquidate and could yield a good price, but what is the emotional cost to you? Remember, handling money is an emotional activity. You don't need to pile negative emotions on top of your financial crisis because you impulsively sold an irreplaceable item.

3. Add to Cash Flow

One of the ways to deal with a higher expense is to match it dollar for dollar with higher income. Even if you can't match it, any additional cash flow will help to keep you from falling into a bottomless debt pit. You may have to put off the Monday night football games and Saturday cookouts. Recognize that a catastrophic expense will entail some sacrifice from your entire family. It might mean missing your son's baseball game once in a while. It is better for your children's well-being for you to miss a little time at home than to allow your family to be saddled with a load of debt.

This is the time to add a second or even third job to your schedule. Don't get too picky if you don't find the perfect job. Find a nice coffee shop and enjoy the benefits of great coffee and fun customers while adding a few dollars to your income. Be careful about starting a new business to generate more income, though. Starting a new business is often a stressful and costly endeavor, and the last thing you need after a catastrophic expense is more stress and expenses! If this is a family affair, some other family members may need to pull more of the load. Does your spouse or child have a unique skill that can add more to the family finances than you are able to? Let them pitch in, and you might even find that the experience draws your family closer together.

● CHATTER BOX **Rick**

I was blessed to have parents who encouraged me to make money on my own. I didn't come from a family of wealth, but we learned to live within our means. When I went to college, I really didn't want to graduate with a pile of student loan debt. For most of my time at school, I worked two outside jobs and sometimes added one job at the university. Assuming that the statute of limitations on auto moving violations has passed, I'll admit that there were times when I would leave class and change into my work uniform while driving down the highway. It wasn't too tricky until I got to the pants. All joking aside, the point is that working multiple jobs isn't exactly the easy life. Nevertheless, if you're willing to put in the hard work, you'll have more money to attack the expense that attacked you.

4. Loans and Relief

Natural disasters often qualify you for special loan assistance. For example, the Small Business Administration (SBA) provides low-interest disaster loans to homeowners and renters to repair or re-place real estate and personal property that have been damaged or destroyed in a declared disaster. There are other disaster relief orga-nizations, including the Federal Emergency Management Agency (FEMA), the Salvation Army, and the American Red Cross.

If you need to get a loan to help you through the catastrophic ex-pense, then make sure you get the best terms. A credit card might be an easy source of funding, but it is one of the most expensive choices. A better choice is to take out a home equity loan or borrow from your 401(k). We don't suggest a retirement account loan lightly, because there are tax penalties associated with such early withdrawals. Taking money from your retirement savings should truly be a last resort, but catastrophic expenses sometimes get you to last resorts.

5. Build Reserves Now

Catastrophic expenses are actually relative to your own financial situation. What is a catastrophic expense for one family is an in-convenience to another. Sometimes an expense that should be nor-mal and expected becomes catastrophic because of a lack of planning. For example, most homeowners can expect to replace their roof every fifteen years or so. The cost of replacement can run $10,000 or more. If you're a homeowner and you know that your roof is soon going to need replacement, that cost can become a cat-astrophic expense if you're currently living paycheck to paycheck with no savings.

Whether you have an expected expense on the horizon or not, it's always a good idea to have a reserve fund. Even if you can put away only a few dollars at a time, every dollar you save now is one less that you have to quickly earn after the expense hits. You have to be disciplined to keep the reserve fund for emergencies only. Just because you didn't get hit with a big expense this year doesn't mean that the reserve fund gets turned into a vacation fund.

College Students

1. Student Loans

Student loans have made it possible for many people to get the education that they otherwise wouldn't have been able to afford. Too often, though, student loans are double-edged swords that become a financial albatross for many years after graduation.

The rule with student loans is the same as the rule with other loans. Don't pay with credit what you can pay for with cash. A student loan generally has a lower interest rate than other loans, and it is fairly easy for most students to access. But a student loan is still a loan. It is debt. It is imperative that you evaluate your ability to repay that debt before you accumulate it. Some fields of study have a much higher salary expectation after graduation than others. Don't walk away with the same debt as a medical student if your income potential isn't in the same league.

Student loans are not an inevitable part of the education process. Have you looked at grants and scholarships? What about going into the workforce now and taking your classes at night and on weekends? Sure, you might not make as much money from the start, but you're gaining valuable experience while paying your way through college. Many companies have an education reimbursement program, so you might not have to pay for your education at all! A college degree is essential in today's world, but you need to be sure you achieve it without overburdening your early working years with debt.

2. Revolving Debt

Revolving debt is just another name for month-to-month debt that you add onto your credit cards. The payment due each month is adjusted based on your current balance. Major credit cards and retail store cards are the culprits that you need to watch here. Since many people get their first credit cards when they go to college, many students haven't developed a healthy respect for just how quickly credit card debt can get out of control. The effects of revolving debt are tempered, too, when multiple cards are involved. You get a different sense of debt if you have $20,000 concentrated on one credit card versus spreading that total over half a dozen different cards.

Students have to be especially wary about revolving debt because they have targets drawn on them by the credit companies. The credit card issuers know that students are in the formative stages of developing spending habits that may last a lifetime. They are well aware of the fact that when students leave the family nest, they begin to develop their own brand loyalties. If a credit card company can hook a student at this stage, the chances are very good that the student will continue to use the card long after graduation. For that reason, credit companies market aggressively to students. You'll often find their sales reps working college bookstores and common areas. Anyplace students tend to congregate, you'll find that the credit marketing isn't far away.

Students must be careful to use credit cards only when necessary. Even if they have the money, it's best that they not use it for convenience' sake until they have a few more years to develop their spending habits. Credit cards create an emotional buffer between your money and the purchase. Using plastic doesn't have the same emotional impact as writing a check or paying cash. For students, that emotional impact is a good thing. It reinforces the fact that the items they are buying come at a cost—not just at the swipe of a card through the machine.

3. Cars

Students haven't been driving more than a few years, and the thrill of the right set of wheels is still strong. Resist the urge to make your ride into a status symbol. A student who sinks into debt to drive around in a car she can't afford is telling the world she doesn't have good money sense. When you're in college, your car is a utility vehicle. Its sole function is to reliably transport you to your classes, work, and other destinations. If you don't tame the beast, your car will begin to control you as you pay for the myriad accessories: audio system, GPS, performance wheels, exhaust kits, and window tinting.

Some students received their starter car when they were sixteen, and college is the time to upgrade. That's fine. You can upgrade without going overboard. Shop around for a reliable used car that has enough good years left to get you through school. You certainly don't want a clunker that will eat up your savings in repair costs or leave you stranded on the highway. Unfortunately, many male students regard their cars in the same way a peacock regards his tail feathers—with an eye toward the peahen. Take the high road and show them how attractive it is to be debt free!

4. Daily Expenses

Most students don't have weighty financial obligations. Usually, there are no mortgages, business obligations, or children to provide for. So students must be diligent about managing the day-to-day expenses. This is the best time to start a personal budget because the budget at this stage will be relatively simple. The key point is that the financial habits that are developed now will influence you for the rest of your life. Develop the right habits early, and you won't have to spend the time and energy to fix them later. After you've read through the Family Budget guidelines in the workbook, review those chapters every few months. The reason for the review is that, as you grow and learn, you will pick up new points that you missed the first time around.

The newfound sense of personal freedom that many students experience when they go off to school can lead to carelessness with money. You get to make the choices about where to eat, when to play, and how much to spend. Just understand that with those choices come responsibilities. It's okay to go out and have some fun. We're not suggesting that you live a life of monklike self-denial. If you do that, you'll probably end up rebelling against yourself. Rather, enjoy your college years, but do it responsibly. Give yourself an allowance and have fun within those boundaries. If you work extra hard and get a bonus, take some of the bounty and reward yourself but also put some of it in your savings or investments (see next section). Through it all, take the time to congratulate yourself for paying attention to the details of managing your personal budget with care.

5. Save Now

Students have an enormous advantage over the rest of the investing world: time. Einstein said, "The most powerful force in the universe is compound interest." The sooner you begin to save, the further along you will be when you need the money for retirement or special circumstances. In the same way that you should develop spending discipline now, you also should develop saving discipline.

One of the simple but powerful principles of saving is the rule of 72. This rule tells you how often your money will double in a savings account. Take the number 72 and divide it by your annual interest rate. The result is the number of years it takes for you to double your money. Here's a simple example. Suppose you have $1,000 in a savings account that earns 10 percent interest each year. Dividing 72 by 10 equals 7.2. In 7.2 years, you'll have $2,000 in your account. Now you can see why it's so important to start saving early. The earlier you start, the more time you have for the rule of 72 to work for you!

Divorce

1. Financial Counseling

We'll start this discussion with the possibility that you are near divorce but not quite there yet. Considering that money problems of various stripes are often cited as a cause of breakups and divorce, it

isn't a bad idea to add this aspect of counseling to any other relationship counseling that you're receiving. It's amazing that couples
get as far as they do in marriage without more significant problems
when you consider how little planning and communication take
place prior to marriage. Two individuals with separate accounts and
unique money habits suddenly come together and try to operate in
unity. *E pluribus unum* sounds good on currency, but it doesn't always work out in marriages. It's no wonder that money issues usually spring up in failing marriages.

If your marriage is still intact, however fragile, make every effort to really fix the underlying issues rather than apply bandages
to the symptoms. We recognize that we're close to venturing beyond our expertise here, but we've worked with enough couples
over the years to know that conflicts about money can be major
contributors to conflicts about communication, trust, and other issues. So in your last-ditch efforts to salvage your marriage, make
sure you don't overlook the one area that might be fueling the fires
of discord—your finances.

2. The Cost of Fighting

Assuming that you've passed the point of no return and the divorce
is in process, your next consideration is settling the divorce as
quickly and efficiently as possible. The bottom line with divorce
proceedings is this: Fighting is expensive. The only person who really makes out well financially in a bitter divorce fight is the attorney. The splitting couple is usually left with crumbs and ashes.

There are no two ways about it—divorce is an emotionally
charged process. There are hurt feelings, betrayed trust, and much
more that can leave one or both parties looking for revenge or jus-
tice. As hard as it may be, you both need to agree to settle as much
as possible without a knockdown fight. We know that this is often
easier said than done, but it should be an objective that you work
toward. That's true with many tough decisions that you have to
make about finances. Remember that this book is about taking

charge of your money, not taking revenge on your spouse. If you want to have any money to take charge of, you need to do your best to minimize the financial impact of a divorce.

There is an approach commonly known as *collaborative divorce*. Just as the name implies, the parties agree to collaborate on a settlement rather than fight through the process. In war, this would be the same as negotiating terms of peace. Both sides agree to lay down arms and work toward an acceptable settlement. The lawyers in a collaborative divorce help the two sides with details and make sure the settlement is clearly understood and enforced.

3. Hiring a Certified Divorce Financial Analyst (CDFA)

There are some special financial situations in which you can go it alone and do well, but there are others that necessitate a little extra help. Since divorce entails so many financial, legal, and emotional challenges, you might do well to consider a financial professional who understands the nuances of divorces. The Institute for Divorce Financial Analysts (IDFA) has created a special designation for financial professionals who specialize in divorce financial planning. Certified Divorce Financial Analysts (CDFAs) are individuals who have met certain requirements that allow them to provide special counsel to people undergoing divorce.

A CDFA can help you make the right decisions early in the divorce process so that you don't pay the penalty down the road, as well as helping you understand the financial ramifications of the divorce settlement and assisting you with planning a postdivorce budget. The longer you wait to get your feet back on the ground after a divorce, the further behind you'll fall in your ability to take charge of your money.

4. Closing Joint Accounts

One of the areas that people neglect in the course of a divorce is the joint accounts held by the couple. We're not just talking about checking or investing accounts here. You also have to consider joint service accounts such as gas, phone, and electric as well as joint loans. You need to avoid adding to your troubles after the divorce settlement by having your ex-spouse run up a debt that has your name attached to it.

Some of the joint accounts may have been open so long that you have forgotten that they were part of your financial picture. To help you with this, here's a checklist of some of the more common accounts that you may need to consider:

- Checking
- Savings
- Brokerage
- Credit cards (including gas and retail)
- Mortgages
- Cars
- Home equity loans or lines of credit
- Safe deposit box
- Utilities
- Phone

How you handle the closing of the joint accounts may be dictated by the terms of the divorce settlement, but your job is to make sure there are no loose ends that need to be tied up.

5. Building Personal Credit

This point is particularly important for a wife who has not been in the workplace. Has your husband been the breadwinner and established a credit history with you jointly named on the accounts? After a divorce, you need to make sure that you have the financial foundation to build on, and a credit history is an important part of that foundation. If you need to get a loan for a house or car, it will be your name and credit history that the lender will review. If you don't have a credit history, then you might miss out on the loan or have to live with less-than-favorable terms.

Building personal credit is the same for those who are just completing the divorce process as it is for young people who are beginning their financial journey. You need to start to use credit a little at a time and pay off your debts when they are due. Open a credit card account and pay the balance in full each month. Start gas or electric service in your name, and make sure that your payments never arrive late. Don't apply for too many credit cards, as this brings your credit score down, but use the credit you have consistently and with discipline. In a short time, you will establish a track record with your credit that lets lenders know that you are someone they can trust.   .

Foreclosure

1. Contact Your Lender

For many people, the home is the single biggest investment in their portfolio. To stand on the brink of losing that investment is more than a financial loss; it's a very personal and emotional loss. Compounding the loss of the home are the additional time and expenses that go along with a forced move and relocation.

If you are facing a foreclosure notice, your first step should be to contact your lender's loss mitigation department. Their role is to mitigate—read "minimize"—losses to the lending institution. Filing a foreclosure and working through the process is time consuming and expensive for lenders. They would much prefer not to have to go through that with you, but they can't work with you toward a solution unless and until you contact them to inform them of your situation. Loss mitigation departments can help you restructure your payment plan without the need to go through a new loan application and underwriting. This may be a short-term catch-up solution if you're experiencing temporary financial difficulties, such as a job transition. Or they may work with you to renegotiate the terms of the loan itself. Many times they can also assist you in finding a third-party debt counseling service to help you create a budget and financial plan to see you through your money storm.

2. Don't Keep the Toys and Lose the Toy Box

This may be hard for you to hear if it applies to you, but sometimes people spend too much money on stuff and then end up losing the real valuables. Recently we helped a friend move from his house after he received a foreclosure notice. When we arrived, there were about a dozen other friends gathered to help. Moving everything out of the house still took almost a week. Do you see something wrong with this picture, too?

Take a long, hard look at your cash flow to understand why you've fallen so far behind in your mortgage payments. Is your mortgage payment vying for priority with your credit card? Are there purchases that are being carried on your credit card balance that could be sold in order to raise cash to pay down your credit cards? What about the cable or satellite service? We've talked to many people who have five hundred channels but not five hundred dollars.

In the "Catastrophic Expense" section, we warned against the danger of fire sales. The same applies here, but that doesn't mean you should hold on to the small stuff while you lose the big stuff. As you're going through your finances looking for ways to stave off foreclosure, take the time to go through your closets. You might find that you can simplify your life while cleaning house. And in the process, you may very well end up keeping the house!

3. Don't Pay Living Rates for Storage Space

They're sometimes called "McMansions"—the oversized, middle-class homes that sit like bloated dwellings on subdivision lots. You can find them by the thousands in suburban neighborhoods, and they are the habitation of choice for millions of young couples. It has become commonplace for these people, fresh out of school, to buy a McMansion that stretches their budget to its breaking point. Unfortunately, without the time to build a reserve fund, any interruption in the cash flow breaks the couple's budget, and then they face the dreaded foreclosure notice.

You can trace the root of the problem back to the fact that a young couple simply doesn't need five thousand feet of living space with four bedrooms and three bathrooms. This is the stepped-up version of buying the fancy car that you couldn't afford in college. Young couples aren't the only ones who are susceptible to this siren song. Many families see the so-called American dream portrayed in the media as the expansive yard and the towering rooflines of a wonderful home. How often have you seen a fiscally responsible family building their wealth debt free while living in a double-wide trailer? It just doesn't have the same marketing appeal, does it?

If your goal is to take charge of your money, then evaluate your housing *needs,* not your housing *wants.* Too many people pay premium mortgage rates for closets and unused rooms. If you really think you need all that space, then consider whether it's being used for people or for things. If you have closets and rooms full of your possessions, it would be better to downsize your home and rent a storage unit than to lose your home entirely. If you have extra rooms that get used only when friends and family visit, it might make more sense to downsize and get your visitors a hotel room when they visit you. As difficult as it may be to admit, your foreclosure might simply be the expected result of biting off more than you can chew—and more than you need to chew.

Our parents and grandparents rented until they could buy a house they could afford. Then they saved their money until they could afford a bigger place that was better suited to their family's needs. Sometimes they stopped there, living their retirement years in a modest ranch house with a manageable yard. If you're riding the status express train that requires you to live house-rich but cash-poor, then jump off now and take charge of your money!

4. Don't Get Hit Twice

For most people going through the ordeal of a foreclosure is a completely new experience—the filings, the phone calls, the reports are all coming at you for the first time. Since you are the novice in a foreclosure, anyone who acts like they can speak the language and work the system will look like an expert. Now is the time to be especially vigilant. Don't fall prey to a foreclosure scam while you're fighting to save your house and finances.

The basis of a foreclosure scam is that it appears to be coming to your rescue. You're at the end of your rope, and they show up to toss you a lifeline. Just what you need, right? Wrong! You may have a guardian angel, but it's highly unlikely that he'll appear to you with a checkbook at the very moment you need to cover your mortgage. The Federal Home Loan Mortgage Corporation (Freddie Mac) has provided a checklist of warning flags to watch for:

- Being approached by a stranger with an unsolicited "rescue" offer
- Receiving an unsolicited call, mail, or flyer about "foreclosure rescue" or saving your home
- Participating in a complicated deal that you don't fully understand
- Signing documents that have blanks or false statements—regardless of what you are told, this is never okay

Don't become paranoid and reject all offers of assistance. Just use your good judgment and know that there are unscrupulous people who will target you in your moment of weakness. Recognizing that, because of the financial stress, your judgment might not be as sharp as usual, ask a trusted friend or family member for an opinion when one of these offers comes to you. Another set of eyes will help you see the red flags you might otherwise miss.

5. Cash-Flow Your House

As we mentioned earlier, many homeowners who find themselves in dire financial straits have more house than they need. If you are in a foreclosure storm and you have extra space, then consider renting out some of the extra room. You don't need to turn your house into a hotel, but there are many opportunities to explore here. This is particularly true if you have segregated space such as a mother-in-law suite, basement, or finished garage.

Use prudence in your selection if you choose to cash-flow your house. You don't want your dream home to become a nightmare because your new tenant is a nut. However, there are many college students, young professionals, widows, and others who could do very well renting space in another family's home. If you don't feel comfortable making that announcement through the city classifieds, then pass the word at your church, doctor's office, or other local network where you live and work.

Identity Theft

1. Detect Early

There is a New Testament parable that teaches that "the man who does not enter the sheep pen by the gate, but climbs in by some other way, is a thief and a robber" (John 10:1, NIV) Throughout history, the thief's advantage is the ability to work undetected. That's why he "climbs in by some other way." The longer the thief has before the alarm is sounded, the more he can steal from you and the greater the damage. One of your best defenses against identity theft is recognizing exactly when the thief has attempted to climb into your finances.

One of the best ways to secure your financial house against identity theft is to closely monitor your credit report. See page 161 for a discussion of how to get your credit report. The major credit bureaus have easy-to-use programs that allow you to access your credit report on demand to view any activity and changes to your report. You can also set alerts based on your preferences that will immediately notify you when an alert is triggered. For example, you can receive an alert if a new account is opened in your name, if your credit balance increases by a predetermined amount, or if there are changes to your public records.

In addition to monitoring your credit report, you need to stay on top of your other account statements. Reconcile your credit card statement with your charge slips. Thieves often post small charges that tend to get overlooked. If you don't recognize a charge on your statement, don't shrug your shoulders and let it pass. That's what people do when they don't take charge of their money.

2. Contact Your Creditors Immediately

If you discover that your security has been breached and someone has stolen your identity, you must aggressively protect yourself. Your first round of calls should be to your creditors. Start with your credit cards, since these are easy targets for thieves. You will likely need to close all of your credit card accounts and reopen accounts with new numbers and passwords. The credit companies will work with you to quickly transfer balances and shut down the compromised accounts. Next contact your bank, broker, and other creditors such as your mortgage company. Let them know that you have become the victim of identity theft, and get their assistance in protecting your accounts with them.

Through the Fair Credit Reporting Act (FCRA), you have the ability to block any information from your credit report that might be the result of identity theft. As you work with your creditors, watch for any activity that comes from the thief. If the thief has already contacted your creditors, you are entitled to submit a written request for copies of the fraudulent applications or records. Your creditors will want to help you clear up the situation, and they're legally required to do their part.

3. Security Freeze

Someone has stolen your identity and wants to take charge of your money. Your objective is to stop that from happening. That scenario is played out in the United States more than eight million times each year. Contact the credit bureaus and initiate a security freeze as soon as you find out that your identity has been stolen. A security freeze locks down your credit report so the thief cannot access it for a new account or application. If the thief attempts to buy a new car with your name, the dealership will not have access to your records and will deny the attempt. Only you can reopen your credit file after providing the required security information to the credit agencies.

Keep in mind that a security freeze only protects against new accounts. If the identity thief has access to your existing accounts, you need to take different steps to protect them. As we mentioned, contact the companies with whom you have existing accounts and make sure you have a protection plan in place.

4. Create a Recovery Diary

Be prepared for a long road to recovery if your identity has been stolen and the thief had a big head start before you discovered the theft. In order to take back control of your personal life, including your money, you're going to have to repair the damage that's been done. You will probably have debts that have been attached to your name, and there will be bill collectors knocking at your door. Many of these collectors are in the business of closing as much debt as possible for their clients. With that objective, their level of customer service is inversely related to their effectiveness. The best bill collectors often have the bedside manner of Scrooge (with all due apologies to Dickens's character).

A recovery diary is invaluable as you straighten out the mess caused by the identity thief. You should keep written records of every phone call, including the number called, date and time of call, whom you spoke with, and the topics discussed. Your diary should have copies of every piece of written correspondence that you sent or received. Anything that includes details that might come in handy as you work through the cleanup should become part of your diary. As a side benefit, you'll find that the creditors and bill collectors will become more helpful when they realize that you're on top of your game and won't be easily dismissed or pushed around.

5. Remember the Minor Accounts

Your first inclination when you realize that your identity has been stolen is to protect the major accounts, such as your checking account and credit cards. That's a good idea, but don't stop there. Make a checklist of all the various accounts and services that you've opened and walk through them one step at a time. These are some of the accounts that you may have overlooked:

- Utilities—gas, electric
- Mobile phone
- Subscriptions—cable, satellite, online services
- Unused open lines of credit
- Retail store or gas cards

Remember that we opened this section by pointing out that thieves prefer to operate undetected. Sometimes they won't storm the gates if they can nibble away at your money without your noticing. If you see a blip in your mobile phone bill or a new monthly charge appears on your credit card, find out where it came from, and you'll be the one in charge of your money.

Job Loss

1. Managing Emotions

With the turmoil in the economy, the chances are better than ever that you have been or will be faced with a job loss. Whether you're fired, laid off, downsized, right-sized, or swept out the door when your company folded, you find yourself without work. There are myriad resources available to help you with the job search process, many of them much better suited to the task than we are. Our goal in this section is to identify key areas that you need to address to help you take and keep charge of your money in the midst of unemployment.

We've said many times that dealing with money is an emotional activity. We tend to feel our way through managing our finances rather than think our way through. If you want to take charge of your money when you're out of work, you have to take charge of your emotions. We're not suggesting for a minute that you deny your emotions or steel yourself against feeling anything. What we're saying is that you have to let your emotions run their course without letting them run your life.

Some studies have suggested that when you lose your job, you can go through a kind of grieving process, which may include denial, anger, bargaining, depression, and acceptance. We've talked to many people over the years who have lost their jobs, and, while we can't state empirically that everyone experiences all of these emotions, we certainly have anecdotal evidence of some of them. We're not qualified to tell you how to work through your grief, so we'll simply tell you that, in our experience, these emotions are normal and almost always temporary. Don't make long-term money decisions while you're in short-term recovery mode.

2. Health Insurance

One of the biggest financial concerns that accompanies a job loss is the issue of health insurance. The media reports have trumpeted story after story about families who apparently teeter on the brink of ruin because of their lack of health insurance. While the evening news may live on hype, you need to address the very real concern about protecting your family against burdensome medical bills. You'll need to decide what to do about health insurance while you're involved in the job search.

Since 1986, most employees have the option of continuing existing health coverage through a provision known as COBRA (Consolidated Omnibus Budget Reconciliation Act). This basically allows you to maintain your existing health plan for up to eighteen months after you lose your job. You continue to receive the group rates and benefits that you received while employed; however, you are responsible for paying the entire insurance premium.

Don't automatically assume that the COBRA option is the best choice for you. There are a number of flexible health insurance plans that can be tailored to your family's needs. You can often eliminate certain coverage such as dental or vision and reduce the monthly premium. You can also assume a higher deductible and copay and drop your premium even further. The point here is that most people have become accustomed to abrogating to their employer the responsibility for health insurance. Now that you're taking charge, start shopping!

3. Less Beats Nothing

The obvious effect of losing your job is having your income stream dry up. If you have a severance package, that may buy you some time for job hunting. During your quest for work you must continually balance your need for search time with your need for an income. One of the ways that you can maintain control over your finances during a period of unemployment is to accept transitional work that may not be up to your normal standards of income. If you have a choice between waiting for the perfect job and accepting something a few notches lower on the food chain, go with the latter for now.

Be sure to watch for future opportunities as well as current income. Too many people think that a cardinal rule of employment is that each successive position must pay at least as much as the previous position. That's a fallacy that has kept many workers from reaching their potential. Sometimes the best move you can make for your career is to take a few steps backward. That might mean accepting an entry-level position in a company where you have more room and opportunity to grow through the ranks. Sometimes it means leaving your comfort zone and learning a new trade or skill that is more marketable in the current economic environment. Along with the lower income comes a need to adjust the family budget.

4. Retirement Accounts Are for Emergencies

You may have heard about the mythical Social Security lockbox, an inviolable account that holds the vast accumulation of Social Security money in the U.S. Treasury. Of course, you realize that such a lockbox doesn't exist except in theory. But the idea isn't a bad one to apply to your own finances. You should consider your own retirement accounts as sitting in a lockbox that can be opened only in the event of a true emergency. Something like the "break glass, pull handle" instructions for fire alarms.

Losing your job doesn't give you a free pass to start raiding your own storehouse. Besides the fact that you will lose your tax-advantaged earnings, taking money from your retirement account costs you both taxes and penalties for early withdrawal. If you intend to take charge of your money, you need to hold yourself accountable to your savings plan, which includes your retirement money. There are many other options to pursue before this last-resort measure is taken. Even a loan against your retirement account is often better than spending the money outright. You have an obligation to repay the loan, and you tend to prioritize that higher since you have a debt to yourself. If you spend retirement funds, you can't redeposit the money when you get back on your feet.

5. Hunt Like You're Hungry

One of the dangers of being responsible with your money and actually having a reserve fund when you lose your job is that you might not be as hungry as someone without a backup account. Just because you can afford to cruise through the job search doesn't mean you should. You've been disciplined up to now; don't lose the advantage. Act like you can eat only what you kill, and go out with focus and energy and find work.

Remember that taking charge of your money is highly dependent on habits that you build and cultivate. Don't allow yourself to fall into the trap of doing less than your best. Always stop and ask yourself whether you've made your best effort to find work or create a new income stream. It's been said that Admiral Hyman Rickover once grilled former U.S. president Jimmy Carter about his education and training, prior to Carter's being admitted to the Navy's nuclear submarine program. When the questioning was over, Admiral Rickover looked Carter in the eye and asked him, "Did you do your best?" Carter said that he had done his best, but then paused and admitted that he hadn't. Admiral Rickover simply asked, "Why not?" Have *you* made your best effort to take charge of your money? If not, why not?

Marriage

1. Fairytale Weddings

If you don't have access to a royal treasury, don't have a wedding and honeymoon fit for a prince or princess. Many newlyweds figure that the wedding and honeymoon are once-in-a-lifetime events. We hope that's true. But that doesn't justify paying for them for the rest of your lifetime. Plan your wedding ceremony according to your means. There are many creative ways to include friends and family in your special day without feeding and housing them as if you were the quartermaster for a standing army. This has the same effect as runaway student loans. You are starting the race of life with an anchor chained to your leg if you accumulate excessive debt from your wedding. It is fashionable to hire wedding planners, organize grand dinners, and bring in your second cousin twice removed from Poughkeepsie. Make it memorable, but carefully count the cost.

The honeymoon is the second part of the package that needs to be controlled. The idea of the honeymoon is to let the newlyweds spend some time celebrating their new life together and getting to know each other. Most people can accomplish that in a quiet cabin in the Great Smoky Mountains as well as they can in a Tahitian cabana. The difference between the two lies in how long you have to make payments on the experience. It would be far better to enjoy a modest honeymoon and save toward an anniversary celebration trip than to sink yourself in debt from the starting line.

2. Dump the Dupes

Now that you have been united in marriage, you need to be united in finances. Let's state up front that there might be legitimate reasons for maintaining some separation of accounts and finances. We'll leave those exceptions for another discussion. For most couples, finances have to be dealt with in a unified manner and with a common purpose. Money hits too close to the heart to expect to have a marriage of the heart with a separation of the pocketbook.

The first step is to review which accounts each individual brings to the marriage and decide what accounts you need to establish together. Many couples open joint accounts, which give the husband and wife equal ownership and access to the funds. Of course, retirement accounts are always individually owned, so it isn't possible to combine those. Beyond that, you need to decide whether each of you will have your own discretionary account. This is often helpful if one spouse is less fiscally responsible than the other. Maintain a family account, but have a separate account that the less-than-responsible partner uses for discretionary shopping. That way, the primary family account won't be raided for a 50 percent off sale.

You should also decide where you'll keep your banking and investing accounts. Take the time to evaluate account options. One partner might have picked a bank with a convenient location. The other might have used a credit union available through his or her employment. Now that you have a new life and financial goals, find the company that best helps you meet those goals.

3. House Rich, Cash Poor

We touched on this subject in the "Foreclosure" section. As a newlywed, make sure you're buying or renting the house you need and can afford. The rule of thumb is that you should get a starter house, not a starter mansion. Here's a good checklist to help you make the right housing selection:

- *How much space do you need for living?* It's better to buy a smaller house and rent storage space if necessary.

- *Watch the taxes.* Tax rates vary among counties and locales, and this can mean the difference between a lot more or a lot less house for the same monthly payment.

- *Choose old over new.* Consider putting "sweat equity" into a fixer-upper house if you have the skills.

- *Be prepared to move often.* Young couples can stay flexible. Don't gold-plate your first home with extensive upgrades unless you are certain to be there for a while, since you won't get your money back when you sell.

- *Rent versus own.* This is the classic choice between the cost of buying and missing out on the opportunity to build equity. Take the time to evaluate this point carefully.

Your home is going to be one of your first big investment decisions. How you deal with this decision sets the stage for how you deal with other money decisions. Make the right choice here, and set in motion the habits that will serve you well for the rest of your life.

4. Set Your Budget Discipline

You can't teach an old dog new tricks. How many times have you heard that conventional wisdom? The message it conveys is that it's difficult to overcome ingrained habits and behaviors. Since that tends to be true, start working with a family budget before you become an "old dog"! The habits that you choose to reinforce at this stage of your life will become second nature as you get older. When you ask couples who are nearing retirement age what they could change about their finances, one of the common answers is "I wish I had started earlier." Well, you now have the opportunity to start earlier.

Don't try to get it all right from the start. Setting your expectations too high only sets you up for failure, and then you give up trying to do anything. Start with the simple things and build as you grow. Use the budget planning guide in the *Take Charge of Your Money Now! Workbook* to help you build and follow a reasonable budget. The primary objective is to recognize the importance of cultivating good money habits early and staying the course. You almost certainly won't appreciate how much you'll benefit from this discipline until you're much older. Take our word for it. The time and energy you invest in your personal money habits now will pay enormous dividends over your lifetime!

5. You're a Team

Marriage is the union of two individuals into one family. You do remember that part of the ceremony, right? Regardless of what you did when you were single, if you want to take charge of your money as a couple, you have to move forward with a common purpose and common goals. Acting like you can be married in heart but not in pocketbook is downright silly. To achieve a union with your finances requires that both of you make the commitment to learn and grow together. This isn't the sole purview of one partner; you're in this together.

Since you'll likely be coming from two different levels of experience and education, a great place to start is with education and training. There are many good classes and seminars available that cover the basics of family finance, debt management, and investing. Take those classes together. It does no good for the husband to let the wife handle the finances and then ignore his responsibility in the matter. Even if the wife handles the checkbook and accounts, the husband must be fully involved in learning and adhering to the budget. Growing separately runs the risk of growing apart. If you grow apart as a couple, then the next section you'll need to read in this chapter is the one entitled "Divorce."

Retirement

1. Working Retirement

Retirement doesn't have to be the endgame of your life. More and more people are finding both satisfaction and financial freedom through retirement careers. The traditional notion of working until you're sixty-five and then striving to match your age to your golf score is not necessarily the best path. By definition, a working retirement entails leaving your career and embarking on a new work path. The new work might be related to your former career, utilizing talents and skills you've built, or it might require starting something completely new.

There are numerous reasons for working into your retirement years if your health allows. The obvious reason, which fits the theme of this book, is the continued income. Many people supplement their Social Security checks or pensions with a working income. A side benefit of many jobs is the health insurance that companies often offer. Add to that the fact that new work and challenges keep the mind and body sharper than idleness, and you make a good case for not dropping out of the workforce entirely.

There are even some careers for which gray hair and wrinkles add to your value. There are many young people who would benefit from your years of experience and learning. If you decide to work at your local coffee shop, stop and think about how many students and young professionals you'll encounter each day. In the course of serving up their morning coffee, you'll likely be able to share your wisdom one nugget at a time.

2. Required Minimum Distributions

You've finally arrived at the stage of life when those years of earnings are ready to be used. The law says that you must take required minimum distributions (RMDs) from your retirement account once you reach a certain age; in most cases, this age is 70$^{1}/_{2}$ years. You need to know up front that if you fail to withdraw your RMD, you can be hit with a significant tax penalty. At this writing, the tax penalty is 50 percent of the RMD amount. If you should have taken $10,000 as your RMD, failure to withdraw the money will cost you a $5,000 penalty. That definitely doesn't fall into the take-charge-of-your-money category!

Calculating the RMD on your retirement accounts is done by referring to the IRS tax tables. This is similar to determining your income tax based on income and filing tables. Your income tax obligation depends on the type of account you used for your retirement savings. A Roth IRA is not subject to income tax, whereas traditional IRAs and company retirement accounts require that you pay income tax on your RMD.

To maintain control over your finances, treat your RMD as you would any other income. RMDs aren't bonuses to be frittered away. If your budget permits, enjoy the RMD, but don't allow yourself to develop negative money habits now. It's a good practice to have a healthy respect for income and expenses at any age, even if the RMD is icing on the cake for you.

3. Don't Juggle Your Nest Eggs

You understand that every investment that takes one dollar and attempts to make it more than one dollar entails some degree of risk.

Some investments have a higher amount of risk because they are expected to generate a higher rate of return. Such is the case with stock market investments as compared to bonds or certificates of deposit (CDs). The expected growth and dividends from investing in individual stocks are offset by the extra risk they carry as compared to CDs.

As you reach your retirement years, you should be moving more of your money away from stocks and higher-risk investments and into more stable investments such as bonds, Treasury notes, and CDs. The reason is simple: If you're living off the income from your investments, you can't afford to suffer large swings in your account value. Some retirees look at their accounts and determine that a conservative income won't meet their needs. As a result, they decide to move to aggressive, riskier investments. That's not an investment strategy; that's a gamble. It might work, but what happens if the investment turns sour? You don't have the years ahead of you to wait for the investment to recover. If your retirement accounts are inadequate to meet your living expenses, then it's better to find ways to cut your expenses and/or add to your income (through a working retirement). The worst idea is to try to make up for lost earnings now by throwing the dice with your retirement savings. More times than not, you end up the loser.

4. Don't Get Scammed

It's difficult to place an accurate price tag on elder fraud, but some studies suggest that scams against the elderly top $40 billion annually in the United States alone. Protecting yourself against con artists is important all through your life, but you need to be extra-vigilant as you get older because the con artists will start targeting you more frequently. Furthermore, many older folks are not as savvy with the Internet and aren't as careful about protecting against online scammers.

The American Association of Retired Persons (AARP) has published a list of the Seven Deadly Scams as a warning about where the scam attacks may originate. Here are some scams to watch out for:

- *Phishing:* You receive an e-mail requesting that you update your personal information for bank accounts, credit cards, and so on. The problem is that the update is fraudulent, and you're tricked into updating your information to a fake website, whereby the scammers get access to your account information.

- *Foreign money offers:* You hold the cash as a favor, and the other party promises to split the cash with you. What do you think they'll be doing with your bank account number?

- *Sweepstakes:* "You may have just won!" . . . but you'll receive your winnings only after you pay the handling or processing fee. The only sure part of this is that you pay the fee.

- *Charity fraud:* The scam takes advantage of your generosity to bilk you out of a generous contribution to the con artist through a nonexistent charity.

- *Foreign lotteries:* "You may have just won!" . . . but in Outer Mongolia. After you send your account information, you'll get the deposit—or so they say.

- *Work at home:* Buy the supplies, and you are promised to make a great home-based income. You get the overpriced supplies and never see the income.

Take Charge and Keep Charge

Now that you're in your retirement years, make sure that the control you have over your finances stays in your hands. Of course, there are times when health or another extenuating circumstance requires that someone else take the reins from you. What we don't want you to do is assume that the friendly financial advisor you met last week is going to care for your money as much as you do. Too often, retired investors start withdrawing from responsibilities that they shouldn't relinquish. Just because you no longer have career responsibilities doesn't mean that you should live a carefree life altogether. Resist the temptation to put your money in someone else's hands and go play.

We've run across more than just a few financial advisors and firms that specifically target older clients. Retired clients tend to have more investment dollars than young investors, and they tend to be more trusting. We actually heard one advisor say that he looks for neighborhoods with white hair and squirrels. The squirrels live in the large oak trees that surround the established homes of retirees. Although this tactic isn't illegal, the motivation behind it often blurs the ethical lines. The fact is, your retirement savings are very attractive to financial advisors. You generally buy what they're selling, and you don't require much of their time.

Don't take this warning as an indictment against every financial advisor who wants your business. There are many respectable advisors who will do a very good job of helping you manage your money. The point is that there are also many who look at you as a source of revenue only. You have to be careful to make a distinction between the two when you're choosing an advisor. In Chapter 5, we discussed some ideas for selecting an advisor. Always stay involved with your investment decisions. Don't yield total control to your advisor, however capable he or she may be.

Starting a Family

1. Save for the Kids Now

You generally have a choice about when you start your family. There's never a perfect time to start a family, but you can take the time to get some of the basics of your family budget in order before your firstborn arrives. It's always good to pay off the wedding and honeymoon, eliminate as much debt as possible, and start building your reserve fund. You don't need to wait until you think you can "afford" children, because many couples don't think they're ever really there.

If you're reading this section and your child is on her way (or already here!), then you still have milestones coming up that you need to start saving for. These may include such things as orthodontia, private schooling, music lessons, and, eventually, college. Time is on your side right now for all of these eventual expenses. If you wait until the event comes along, you'll be scrambling to make ends meet. If you recognize that there will be special occasions that require additional spending, you'll be much better off setting aside a few dollars on a regular basis and letting compounding interest work for you.

A good idea is to have a separate account for each event that you're saving toward. Try to keep the different accounts with the same bank or broker to minimize account expenses. Many financial companies will consider the total value of all your accounts when determining your account fees. The reason for opening separate accounts is that you have a clear picture of your progress in saving for each event. If you mix it all into one account, you lose sight of how much you have versus how much you need for the different events.

2. Prioritize the Budget

Once the bouncing ball of joy shows up in your life, you have to be prepared to make new priorities in your family budget. It's no longer business as usual if you plan to take charge of your money when you change from a two-person household to one with three (or more) members. Young parents sometimes make the mistake of adding the inevitable child expenses without a commensurate reduction of expenses or addition of income somewhere else. You will very quickly settle into a pattern of buying diapers, formula, and all sorts of other necessities.

The biggest mistake you can make is to start adding debt when you add expenses. It may not seem like much to use the credit card to buy the next box of baby wipes, but the purchases add up quickly. Take a close look at your discretionary spending—areas that you didn't pay such close attention to before your child was born. Can you reduce or eliminate expenses such as restaurants, movies, and manicures? Review your budget often to make the necessary adjustments.

3. Working Parents and Day Care

Don't assume that your only financial recourse after your baby arrives is to have both parents working as long and hard as possible. That might be the case, but it should be a decision you make based on your own situation, not a default decision that you haven't fully evaluated. As you evaluate whether both of you should continue working, take into account the financial as well as personal factors. Make sure you consider all aspects of the impact this will have on your family. Here are just some of the costs that come with both parents working outside the home:

- Day care
- Commuting
- Wardrobe—business dress is more expensive
- Auto maintenance
- Insurance
- Higher tax bracket
- Lunch, gifts, office collections

It's a lot easier to figure out the additional income—after taxes, of course. The expenses are a little tougher to fully account for, so make sure you understand the big picture. It may surprise you, but you might do better with one parent staying at home than if both of you work.

4. Life Insurance

You can't drive down the road without car insurance, and your mortgage company won't lend you a dime without insurance on your house. However, you get to bring a new life into the world without any legal obligation to provide for the child beyond your income. If you depart this life, you'd better be insured. That's a basic obligation (legal or not) that you have toward your family. Once you start a family, you need to carefully review the amount and type of life insurance that both parents should carry to protect against financial hardship if your child should lose one or both of you.

This discussion is not meant to be a primer on life insurance; there are plenty of resources to consult for more detail. Recognizing that you need to have life insurance coverage, be sure to factor the premiums into your family budget. Term life insurance is generally the least expensive. Many policies allow you to lock in the terms and rate for a fixed renewal period—sometimes up to thirty years. The amount of insurance you choose—called the *policy face value*—will affect your premiums. It is possible to be overinsured, which leaves you paying for more insurance than you really need. Don't make this decision lightly, assuming that you probably won't ever need the policy. That's probably true, but if you ever do need it, your family will be grateful that you made a wise, informed decision!

5. Baby Gets a Budget

Repeat after me: "I am not a bad parent if I don't buy the best of everything for my child." There are otherwise money-conscious parents who seem to lose all touch with financial reality when it comes to buying for the baby. We never cease to be amazed at the never-ending supply of gadgets and accessories that show up in the baby stores. A cursory review of strollers at a major online retailer shows the price ranging from $19.99 to $999.99! You are not committing child abuse if you don't get the thousand-dollar model for your child.

There are baby items, such as formula and diapers, that might require you to pay a little more. If your child doesn't like the taste of the generic brand of formula, spend a little more for something that goes down more easily. If the cheap diapers leak like a bad faucet, upgrade to a better brand. But you don't have to buy your child a knurled walnut crib and every toy under the sun. It's a lot better to involve children in the family budget right from the start than to fix their tastes later, when those tastes have become even more expensive.

Windfalls

1. Don't Embarrass Drunken Sailors with Your Spending

One of the most important lessons you can teach your children and grandchildren is how to spend money appropriately. When they get their first allowance, the cash suddenly starts to burn holes in their pockets. It doesn't seem to matter what they spend their newfound wealth on, they possess an overwhelming urge to spend. Take them to the store with some cash in hand, and it will pain them to walk back out of the store without having made a purchase of something, anything!

That same tendency arises all over again if you find yourself in the fortunate position of having received a windfall of money. You might have just opened your Christmas bonus from your employer and found out that it was a very good year. You might be one of the few who scratches a ticket and finds the lucky numbers in the lottery. Perhaps you're the recipient of an insurance settlement, inheritance, or judgment. Whatever the source, you have free cash in your pocket and you're right back to being a kid with your first allowance.

Your first challenge is to temper the urge to spend the money. A good idea is to write down the total on a sheet of paper and allocate it according to a budget. From the total, carve out a small portion to splurge on yourself without guilt. Then make a list of how you want to direct the rest of the money. Use the following list to help you cover the important bases:

- Debt payoff
- Tithe and charitable contributions
- Mortgage paydown/payoff
- Retirement savings
- Education savings
- Reserve funds
- Insurance
- Investments

If you take the time to write out a plan for your new money, you'll take an important step toward removing some of the emotion that comes with the cash. Take a breath, make a plan, and you'll look back in a few years without regrets.

2. Protection Beats Growth

We've been a part of a lot of discussions that went something like this: "If I could only get $5 million, I would put it in CDs and live off the interest." Of course, the amount changes from one person to the next, but they're saying the same thing—there's an amount of money that would put an end to their working and striving. If they could reach that number, they'd quit trying to get more. If you've been fortunate enough to hit that number in one fell swoop, then realize that you can move from growth to protection with your investments.

Be on your guard against the tendency to play for double or nothing with your largesse. Some people are sorely tempted with new money because they figure it was "free," meaning that it didn't cost them anything to acquire it so they can take extra chances with it. In fact, there's an entire game built around this: Deal or No Deal. One aspect of the game is the "double-or-nothing" play. After the contestants have accumulated a known amount of money, they are sometimes given an opportunity to double their winnings. They look at the many thousands of dollars in their hand and immediately think about what they would do with twice that amount. We suspect that many fewer players would take the gamble if it was their monthly salary on the line rather than some quick winnings.

A prudent move with a windfall is to place the money in conservative growth investments such as bonds, CDs, and conservative index funds. Don't roll the dice by betting your money on a stock tip or risky business.

3. Friends and Family

Perhaps this section would be better titled "Supposed Friends and Long-Lost Family." We certainly don't want to discourage you from reaching out to your close friends and family members when you have extra resources. What we want to warn you about is the wave of people who will suddenly remember how much you mean to them.

You may be a generous individual, but you're going to have to develop a keen sense of when to say no. You'll probably hear some pretty compelling cases from people who think that your duty is to extend your good fortune to them. In almost every case, it is not your duty. Whether you choose to assist someone in need is your decision and should be based on a true evaluation of need rather than guilt. This is one reason that wealthy individuals establish foundations and strict giving plans. Without guidelines and discipline, you can imagine how a wealthy person would be constantly bombarded by requests for help. Your new wealth places you in the precarious position of having big money without big money experience.

Once again, a good course of action is to create a budget and stick to it. If you choose to allocate 10 percent of your money toward helping friends and family in need, then stop when you've doled out 10 percent. However much you choose to give away, make sure that you have a process for sorting the legitimate requests from the beggars. This is one area where the counsel of a couple of trusted friends comes in handy. It doesn't require an attorney and a tax professional to give you some good perspective; the advice of some well-grounded friends goes a long way here.

4. Professional Advice

It's quite possible that your windfall will bring new financial considerations into your life. You might not have given much thought to such issues as estate planning, tax planning, and advanced investments, but you should consider how to address them now. Many of these issues are sufficiently complex as to require the help of someone with specialized training.

Your first call should be to a qualified financial advisor. Besides helping you with your current budget and investments, the right advisor will have a network of tax and legal professionals. He or she will refer you to some others who can address your specific requirements. Don't look for the cheapest person when shopping for an advisor. Take the time to interview a prospective advisor's other clients and referrals and find someone who will invest the time you need.

5. Protect Your Children

Warren Buffett, one of the wealthiest and most successful investors in the world, said that he will not leave his entire fortune to his children. According to *Fortune* magazine, he does not intend to give them "a lifetime supply of food stamps just because they came out of the right womb." Buffett wants his children to learn the value of hard work and earning money, and he believes that giving them too much is a corrupting influence.

Take the Buffett lesson to heart with your own children if you receive a financial windfall. Just because you can afford to buy your kids the best of everything now doesn't mean that you should actually do it. You need to instill in your children the values and habits that will serve them well throughout their life, rich or poor. You don't necessarily have to become a miser and selfishly take care of your own affairs without assisting your offspring at all. However, they will certainly not learn to value that which comes too easily.

Think of yourself as an employer, and imagine that your children work for you. Come up with chores and responsibilities for them and then reward them with a generous allowance. Better yet, encourage them to start a business and provide them with some seed capital. Don't make it too much or they'll lose the connection between work and reward, but allow them to participate in the windfall through their efforts. Through it all, consider the characteristics you want your children to possess if they should ever be in a tight financial situation.

Take Charge Like the Pros!

The world of professional finance is nothing if not new and unknown. When stock options were introduced to the markets, very few traders knew what to do with them. The traders who survived and thrived were those who took the time to learn about options and how they changed the game. They didn't necessarily trade options in their own accounts, but they didn't ignore them as if they didn't exist. The markets and financial businesses are constantly changing and presenting new challenges and opportunities. You'll never find successful professionals lamenting the way things used to be and pretending that business goes on as usual.

If you are going to take charge of your money, you have to act like the pros. You need to handle unexpected circumstances with a resolve to learn and grow from them. You need to attend to the details that will let you come out on the other side stronger and more confident. As always, the spoils do not go to the smartest, they go to the most diligent and disciplined. Resolve now to be the most diligent and disciplined and be ready to take charge of your money—even through the unexpected!

ACKNOWLEDGMENTS

The Market Guys couldn't continue on our mission without the help and support of our family, friends, and associates. Together, we have to start by recognizing Bob Marty, who scratched the surface enough to see the diamonds in the coal. The Market Guys had begun building our dream when Bob stepped in and dreamed even bigger. This work reflects his dream and his guidance. Mitchell Waters, our agent at Curtis Brown, brought this book to the marketplace with a speed and efficiency that we couldn't otherwise have imagined. His guidance and efforts were crucial to a successful launch. We are always amazed at the skill of the publishing team. We want to thank Christina Duffy and Jane von Mehren, at Random House, for their guidance and suggestions. This book is a far better product due to their many notes, corrections, and ideas.

Rick:

"Honor your father and mother" is a commandment that is followed with a promise. This book is dedicated to my parents, Watson and Bonnie Swope. From my youth, they cultivated the entrepreneurial spirit within me and taught me the purpose of money. Their many nighttime readings of classics like *The Raggedy Man* and *The Village Blacksmith* forged my lifelong love of poetry and language. My ability to even consider writing a book on finance is the result of their encouragement.

INDEX

account custodian, 70
accountability
    in family budget, 106
    through financial plan, 101
    of Wall Street and Washington,
        144
accounts
    identity theft and, 181
    joint, in divorce, 172–73
    See also specific types
adjustable rate mortgages (ARMs),
    90–91
advertising, conditioned response
    to, 121–23
after-tax dollars, in retirement
    accounts, 52
Air Mobile Ministries, 149
American Association of
    Retired Persons (AARP),
    191
American dream, 17, 176
American Red Cross, 166
anger, power of, 74
annual percentage rate (APR)
    car loans and, 83–84
    credit cards and, 76, 94, 120
annuities, 120
Appel, Max, 123

assets
    catastrophic expenses and, 164
    liquidation of, 157–58, 159
attitude, negative vs. positive,
    35–38, 42–46
auction market, 5
auction websites
    catastrophic expenses and, 164
    selling stamps/coins on, 21
automated teller machines
    (ATMs), 49, 50, 60, 61
automobiles. *See* cars

bailouts by U.S. government, xv
bank accounts
    for children's expenses, 194
    fees for, 60–61
    identity theft and, 179
    joint, 172–73, 186
    number of, 54, 63, 72
    reconciling statements from,
        163
    See also checking accounts;
        savings accounts
Bankrate.com, 57, 128
bankruptcy
    Chapter 7, 157–58
    Chapter 13, 158

bankruptcy (*cont.*)
  of corporations, 141
  credit card debt and, 79
  credit counseling and, 158–59
  overcoming, 161–63
  reason for, 157, 162
  rebuilding credit after, 160–61
  retirement saving and, 158, 159
Bankruptcy Abuse Prevention and
  Consumer Protection Act
  (BAPCA), 159
banks
  failures of, 56
  selecting, 55–63, 72
Barclays, 27
bear markets, 16, 26
Bear Stearns, 56
bill collectors, 180
Billy's Walawi Project, Inc., 148
bonds
  as investments, 30
  in mutual funds, 25
  researching, 62
  in risk management strategy, 70,
   191
  windfalls allocated to, 199
borrowing
  against home equity, 86
  in margin accounts, 51
  See also debt
bottled water industry, 119–20,
  134
brand loyalties, 168
brokerage accounts
  function of, 50–51
  joint, 173
brokerages
  failure of, 57
  selecting, 55–63, 72
  suitability rules and, 136

budget
  for college students, 169, 170
  home size and, 176
  postdivorce, 172
  for windfall funds, 199
  See also family budget
Buffett, Warren, 200
bull markets, 16, 26
buy two get one free deals, 94–95
buyers
  bull markets and, 16
  market function of, 11

Cape McClear (Central Africa),
  148
capital
  boosting, 136
  preserving, 15
  raising via initial public
   offering, 21
  for start-up business, 201
capital gains taxes, 51
cars
  for college students, 168–69
  down payments on, 81–82
  factory invoice price of, 84–85
  insurance on, 195
  joint ownership of, 173
  sign-and-drive deals, 80–81
  trade-in allowances on, 85
  upside-down loans for, 82–83
Carter, Jimmy, 185
cash
  vs. credit, 167
  credit card advances for, 80
  daily saving of, 116
  as emergency fund, 143
  as financial plan component, 68
  generating, for catastrophic
   expenses, 163

vs. gift cards, 95–96
with mortgage refinancing, 86
in risk management strategy, 70
cash accounts (brokerages), 51
catastrophic expenses
   effects of, 163
   health insurance and, 182
   increasing income to meet,
     164–65
   natural disasters as, 165–66
   reserve fund to meet, 166
   selling assets to meet, 164
certificates of deposit (CDs)
   researching, 62
   in risk management strategy, 70,
     191
   windfalls allocated to, 199
certified divorce financial analyst
   (CDFA), 172
certified financial analyst (CFA),
   67
certified financial planner (CFP),
   67
certified market technician (CMT),
   67
Chapter 7 bankruptcy, 157–58
Chapter 13 bankruptcy, 158
charities
   fraud involving, 192
   windfall donations to, 198
checking accounts
   fees for, 61
   function of, 49–50
   joint, 173
   reconciling statements from,
     163
child support, and bankruptcy,
   158
children
   catastrophic expenses and, 165

custodial accounts for, 52–53
education savings for, 53, 159
expenses for, 193–97
family budget and, 105
financial education of, 21, 197
as heirs, 200–1
savings accounts for, 49
simplicity of, 111–12
COBRA health plans, 183
coin collecting, 21
collaborative divorce, 172
college students
   cars for, 168–69
   credit cards and, 167–68
   See also student loans
common stock, 22
community organizations,
   142–43
company stock, risk with, 28–29
complacency, dangers of, 141,
   144
conditioned response, 121
confidence
   building, 20, 31
   of investors, 10, 14, 18
   in money management, 118
   sense of purpose and, 145–46
consideration, defined, 11
Consolidated Omnibus Budget
   Reconciliation Act
   (COBRA), 183
consumer advocacy groups, 159
Consumer Confidence Index, xv
consumer debt, 158
Consumer Federation of America
   (CFA), 112
consumerism
   financial control and, 74–75
   stress and, 112
   See also spending

corporations
  bankruptcy of, 141
  consumer conditioning by,
    121–23
  profit margins for, 120
  shareholder value and, 119,
    122
counseling
  for credit, 158–59
  for debt, 175
  financial, in divorce, 170–71
  about windfall allocation, 199,
    200
coupon, in bond investing, 30
credit
  vs. cash, 167
  overspending and, 143
  postdivorce, 173–74
  rebuilding, 160–61
credit cards
  for disaster loans, 166
  discipline and, 41
  fees/penalties on, 79–80
  financial education and, 21
  interest on, 76–77
  joint, 173
  life insurance through, 77–78
  number of, 78–79, 96–97, 115,
    161, 168, 174
  paying down, 175
  profit margins on, 120
  reconciling statements from,
    163
  revolving debt and, 167–68
  from stores, 76, 93, 161
credit counseling, 158–159
credit history, 173
creditors
  in bankruptcies, 158
  identity theft and, 179

credit report
  identity theft and, 178–79
  obtaining, 161
  security freeze on, 180
credit score
  account applications and, 161
  bankruptcy and, 161
  car sales and, 82, 83–84
  credit cards and, 76, 78, 97,
    174
custodial accounts, 52–53

day care expenses, 195
Deal or No Deal (game), 198
debt
  car sales and, 81, 168–69
  from credit cards, 76, 79, 97
  eliminating, 143
  emotional response to, 74
  in family budget, 101, 108
  having children and, 194–95
  vs. home equity, 86–87
  from identity theft, 180
  postdivorce credit and, 174
  restructuring, 158
  revolving, 167–68
  student loans as, 167
  from wedding, 185–86
  windfalls allocated to, 198
debt counseling services, 175
debt management plan (DMP),
  158
decision making
  catastrophic expenses and, 164
  emotional aspect of, 137
decluttering, 113, 116
Diamond Trust Series (DIA) ETF,
  26
diet, in stress management, 113
disaster loans, 165–66

discipline
   adjustable rate mortgages and,
      90
   in building wealth, 137
   college students and, 170
   with credit cards, 41, 79–80,
      174
   custodial accounts and, 53
   importance of, 104–5
   in marital finances, 188
   in rebuilding credit, 161
   success and, 47, 201
discretionary accounts, 186
diversification
   defined, 29
   with exchange-traded funds, 26,
      28, 70
   by financial advisor, 71
   in financial services companies,
      63, 72
   with mutual funds, 25, 26
dividends
   from common stock, 22
   as income, 23
   from preferred stock, 22
   reinvesting, 23, 24
divorce
   credit and, 173–74
   financial counseling and, 170–71
   joint accounts and, 172–73
   settlement of, 171–72
dollar cost averaging
   for mutual funds, 25
   for stock investing, 24–25
Dow, Charles, 26–27
Dow Jones Industrial Average
      (DJIA)
   drop in (2008), xv
   function of, 26
   index funds and, 61

Dow Theory, 27
down payments on cars, 81–82

Earth Policy Institute, 120
eBay, 11, 21
education
   vs. discipline, 104
   about family finance, 189
   in financial concepts, 109–110
   fiscalcatastrophobia and, 132
   in investing, 11–12, 18
   paying for, 194
   savings accounts for, 52–53,
      159, 198
education reimbursement
      programs, 167
80/20 rule, 156
elderly people, fraud against, 191
emergencies
   cash saved for, 116, 143, 166
   financial plan for, 143, 155–56
emotions
   in car purchase, 81
   catastrophic expenses and, 164
   credit card purchases and, 168
   in decision making, 137
   family budget and, 105, 106
   financial plan and, 101, 134
   home foreclosures and, 174
   in home purchase, 88–89
   impulse buying and, 127
   job loss and, 181–82
   money and, 74, 98, 99
   as stock market driver, 5–6
   of stock traders, 117
   windfalls and, 198
employment
   catastrophic expenses and,
      164–65
   loss of, 181–85

employment (*cont.*)
  student loans and, 167
  windfalls and, 198
  work-at-home scams, 192
Equifax.com, 161
equity in home, 30, 86
equity shares, 20
  See also stocks
estate planning, 200
exchange-traded funds (ETFs)
  diversification via, 70
  for gold, 30
  as investment, 26–28
exit price, 106
expenses
  catastrophic, 163–66
  for college students, 169–70
  in family budget, 101, 103,
    108
  family contributors to, 105
  of having children, 193–97
  See also spending
Experian.com, 161

Fair Credit Reporting Act (FCRA),
  179
families, catastrophic expenses
    and, 164–65
family budget
  children's expenses in, 193–97
  creating, 101
  discipline needed for, 104–5,
    143
  duration of, 107, 188
  goals of, 102–3
  job loss and, 184
  participants in, 105–6
  prepackaged kits for, 103–4
  prioritizing in, 194–95

review of, 107–9, 115, 169
simplicity of, 102
as unique, 109–10
written, 106
Farrelly, Kathleen, 146–48
fear
  of losing money, 132–33
  managing, 130–32, 137
  as stock market driver, 5–6
Federal Deposit Insurance
    Corporation (FDIC), 56, 57
Federal Emergency Management
    Agency (FEMA), 166
Federal Home Loan Mortgage
    Corporation (Freddie Mac),
    177
fees
  account consolidation and, 54,
    194
  on annuities, 120
  for ATM withdrawals, 50
  on car sales, 81, 82
  for checking account
    transactions, 50
  on credit cards, 79–80, 97
  for ETFs vs. mutual funds, 27
  for financial services, 60–61
  on home sales, 87
  for index fund managers, 62
  loads on mutual funds, 136
  to money managers, 48
  for online financial services, 59
  for savings account transactions,
    49
  in sweepstakes scams, 192
  for tax preparation, 55
  tracking of, 75
  on twelve months same as cash
    deals, 94

financial advisors
  retirement and, 193
  selecting, 63–71, 73
  windfalls and, 200
financial crisis of 2008, xv, 56, 69,
    131, 137–38
financial experts, advice from, 15
financial independence, 35–36
financial management, ostrich
    strategy for, 15
financial plan
  accountability through, 101
  checklist for, 115–17
  for emergencies, 143, 155–56
  emotional control via, 134
  goals in, 116–17
  suitability checklist, 136–37
  for windfalls, 197–98
financial products
  researching, 61–62, 127–28
  selection of, 72
  selling of, 64–68
  See also specific products
financial services companies
  as IPO underwriters, 22
  selecting, 55–63, 72
financial statements
  information security and, 62–63,
    179
  online, 59–60
  reconciling, 163, 179, 181
  reviewing, 8, 54, 79, 97
  See also record keeping
fire sales, 164, 175
fiscalcatastrophobia, 132–33
Fitchratings.com, 57
flea circus mentality, 37–38, 41
Forbes (magazine), 11
Forbes.com, 26

foreclosures
  cash flow to prevent, 178
  home size and, 175–77
  loss mitigation in, 174–75
  as property investments, 30
  rescue offers for, 177
  spending rate and, 175
foreign lottery scams, 192
foreign money offers, 192
401(k) plan, borrowing from, 166
franchises, as investments, 30
fraud
  credit card, 79
  of elderly, 191–92
  investor, xv, 70
fund/money managers
  role of, 4, 25
  selecting, 48
  vs. self-management, 47

gift cards, 95–96
gifts, from windfall money, 199
Giving While Living foundation,
    147
goals
  family budget and, 101, 102–3,
    106, 108, 109
  in financial plan, 143
  motivation and, 39, 40–41
  profits as, 133, 134
  S-M-A-R-T, 116
gold
  as investment, 30–31
  price of, 122
good faith estimates (GFEs), 128
grants, for college, 167
greed
  controlling, 134
  fiscalcatastrophobia and, 133

greed *(cont.)*
  investment strategy and, 15,
    132
  as stock market driver, 5–6,
    132
Greenflight International, 150

habits
  in buying, 93
  changing, 161–62, 188
  forming positive, 44
  money management and, 185,
    190
  students and, 168, 169
health insurance
  job loss and, 182–83
  working retirement and, 189
Holders (Merrill Lynch), 27
home equity loans, 166, 173
home ownership
  affordable, 175–77, 187
  builder upgrade costs, 88–90
  cash-back refinancing, 85–87
  closing costs, 87–88, 128
  foreclosures and, 174–78
  as investment, 30
  without mortgage, 15–18
  natural disaster loans and, 166
Home Shopping Network, 123
honeymoons, cost of, 186, 193
hot buttons
  goal achievement and, 39
  for retail spending, 93
hurricanes, profit opportunities
    from, 134
Hurston, Joe, 149

identity theft
  credit cards and, 79, 93, 97
  creditors and, 179

detecting, 178–79
  excess accounts and, 54
  financial institutions and, 62–63,
    72
  recovery diary for, 180–81
impulse buying, 127
income
  from bond investing, 30
  child care expenses and, 195
  in family budget, 101, 103, 108
  family contributors to, 105
  increasing, 164–65
  job loss and, 183–84
  in retirement, 24, 189–91
  vs. spending, 119
  taxable, from dividends, 23
income taxes
  paycheck deductions for, 60
  retirement accounts and, 51
index funds, 61, 70, 199
individual retirement accounts
    (IRAs)
  annual contributions to, 53–54
  real estate investment and, 30
  required minimum distributions
    from, 190
  stock dividends in, 24
  taxes and, 51, 52
  See also Roth IRAs
infomercials, 123–26, 133
initial public offering (IPO), 21–23
Institute for Divorce Financial
    Analysts (IDFA), 172
insurance
  coverage needed, 78, 109
  for financial institutions, 57, 72
  health, 182–83
  life, 77–78, 195–96
  windfalls allocated to, 198
insurance companies, 22

interest
  on adjustable rate mortgages,
    90–91
  on car loans, 83–84, 85
  on certificates of deposit, 62
  from checking accounts, 50
  compound, 170, 194
  on credit cards, 76–77, 79, 80,
    93, 97, 120
  Federal Reserve and, 5
  on margin accounts, 51
  on mortgages, 86, 87–88, 128
  from savings accounts, 49, 170
  on student loans, 167
Internet
  elder fraud on, 191, 192
  financial research via, 128
  financial services via, 55, 58, 72
  information security on, 62–63
  record keeping via, 59–60
investment accounts
  in bankruptcy, 159
  fees for, 60–61
  number of, 63, 72
investment banks, 22
investments
  bonds as, 30
  through brokerage accounts, 51
  choices in, 20, 27–28, 29, 31
  by college students, 170
  exchange-traded funds as, 28
  in family budget, 108
  gold as, 30–31
  index funds as, 61
  limiting losses in, 136
  long-term strategies for, 24–25
  marriage and, 186
  mutual funds as, 25–26
  protecting, 13–14, 17, 18
  real estate as, 30

  in retirement, 190–91, 193
  return on, 133, 134
  risk tolerance and, 135
  seeking advice on, 200
  sense of purpose and, 147–50
  stocks as, 4, 21–25
  suitability of, 68–69, 73, 135–36
  windfalls allocated to, 198, 199
investors
  confidence of, 10, 14, 18, 20, 31
  fear experienced by, 130,
    132–33
  financial awareness of, 73
  fraud against, xiv, 70
  profits/losses and, 70
Investor's Business Daily, 11
irrational exuberance, 5
IRS tax tables, 190
iShares (Barclays), 27

job loss
  · emotional aspects of, 181–82
  health insurance and, 182–83
  job hunting after, 184–85
  retirement savings and, 184
  transitional work and, 183–84
jobs. *See* employment
joint accounts, 172–73

Katrina, Hurricane, 149
Keep It Super Simple (KISS)
  for bank/brokerage accounts, 53
  for family budget, 102, 109
  for financial advisor selection,
    71
  in Market Guys' seminars, 114
  as philosophy, 111, 118

Lehman Brothers, 56
leverage, in investing, 14

life insurance
    credit card, 77–78
    having children and, 195–96
liquidation of assets
    in bankruptcy, 157–58, 159
    catastrophic expenses and,
        163
loan points, 88
loans
    building credit with, 161
    car, 80–84
    home equity, 166, 173
    joint, 173
    natural disasters and, 165–66
    against retirement funds, 184
    See also mortgages; student
        loans
lottery scams, 192
low-APR loans, 83–84
Lucent Technologies, 29

Macken, Tony, 146–48
Madoff, Bernard, 70
mailing lists, removal from, 116
margin accounts (brokerages), 51
The Market Guys
    experience of, xii, 19
    seminars by, 113, 146
The Market Guys' Five Points for
        Trading Success (Monte and
        Swope), xi
market index options, 69
market share, capturing, 119
marketing
    of cars, 80–85
    of credit cards, 76–77, 168
    effectiveness of, 121
    get one free offers, 94–95
markets
    behavior of, 27

bull vs. bear, 16
    demand in, 23
    educating yourself about,
        11–12, 14–15, 18
    function of, 10–11
    language of, 9–10, 14, 18
    respect for, 130
    value drivers in, 134–35
    See also stock market
marriage
    breakups over money, 112,
        170–174
    common financial purpose in,
        188–89
    financial accounts in, 186–87
    home ownership in, 187–88
    honeymoon costs, 186
    wedding costs, 185
    See also divorce; spouse
maturity date
    of bonds, 30
    of certificates of deposit, 62
Mays, William D. (Billy), 123
McMansions, 175–76
Megatrends (Naisbitt), 58
mentoring, 190
Merrill Lynch, 27
money, fear of losing, 132–33
money market accounts, 4
Morningstar, 26
mortgages
    adjustable rate, 90–91
    avoiding, 15–18
    cash-back refinancing, 85–87
    foreclosures and, 174, 175
    insurance and, 195–96
    jointly held, 173
    on new homes, 88–90
    no-closing-cost, 87
    points on, 88

rate comparisons for, 128
windfalls to pay off, 198
motivation
toward goals, 39
lack of, 35–37
pain/pleasure as, 39–40
mutual funds
fees for, 27, 136
function of, 25
investments within, 4
managing, 25
researching, 61–62
trading, 26, 51

Naisbitt, John, 58
National Association of Securities
Dealers (NASD), 135
natural disasters, 165–66
negative-amortization loans,
90–91
negative conditioning, 37, 40, 41
net asset value (NAV), 26
net worth, home ownership and, 30
new-construction homes, 88–90
New York Stock Exchange
image of, 4
suitability rules of, 135

oil price fluctuations, xv
optimism/pessimism, 117–18
Orange Glo International, 123
ostrich investing strategy, 14, 69
overdraft fees, 61

pain, as motivator, 39–41
paper shredders, 62
Pareto principle, 156
passwords
for bank accounts, 62
identity theft and, 179

personal information
from credit cards, 79, 93, 97
in elder fraud, 192
security of, 54, 62–63, 72,
178–81
suitability rules and, 135
phishing, 192
phobias, 131–32
physical health
fiscal health and, 116
pessimism and, 117
stress management and, 112,
113
pleasure, as motivator, 39–41
policy face value, 196
portfolio
diversification of, 30
efficiency of, 27
rebalancing, 108
software for reviewing, 68
Positive Actions diary, 45
preferred stock, 22
profit margins, 120–21
profits
for financial advisors, 64, 67
greed and, 133
as investment goal, 133
opportunities for, 134–35,
143–44
protecting, 13–14, 17, 18
purpose
benefits of finding, 145–46
investing and, 147–48

rating services, 57, 72
real estate
as investment, 14, 30
natural disasters and, 166
See also home ownership; rental
properties

rebates, 91–93

recession
    triggers of, 131
    See also financial crisis of
        2008

record keeping
    for family budget, 108
    fees for, 61
    by financial service, 72
    identity theft and, 179, 180–81
    online, 59–60
    See also financial statements

registered retirement savings plan
    (RRSP), 24

reinvestment of stock dividends,
    23, 24

rental properties
    vs. home ownership, 187
    homes as, to prevent
        foreclosure, 178
    as investments, 30

reorganization bankruptcy, 158

research services
    from financial institutions,
        61–62
    for mutual funds, 26

reserve funds
    for catastrophes, 166
    for children's expenses, 194
    windfall contributions to, 198

retail sales
    of cars, 84
    decline in (2008), xv

retail stores
    buy two get one free deals,
        94–95
    credit cards from, 76, 93, 97,
        161, 167
    gift cards from, 95–96

rebates from, 91–93
    twelve months same as cash
        deals, 94

retirement
    financial control during, 192–93
    fraud and, 191–92
    working during, 189–90

retirement accounts
    bankruptcy liquidations and,
        158, 159
    borrowing from, 166, 184
    company stock in, 28–29
    contributions to, 24
    function of, 51–52
    marriage and, 186
    mutual funds in, 25
    required minimum distributions
        from, 190
    stock dividends in, 24
    windfall contributions to, 198

Rickover, Admiral Hyman, 185

Riordan, Billy, 148

Riordan, Mags, 148

risk management
    through diversification, 29
    evaluating investments in, 136
    financial advisor and, 69–70
    importance of, 160
    in initial public offerings, 22–23
    market familiarity and, 20
    with mutual funds, 25
    by professional investors, 73
    in retirement, 190–91
    in stock investing, 11–15
    of windfalls, 198–99

risk tolerance, 135, 136

Rodante, Doug, 149–50

Roth IRAs, 52, 190

rule of 72, 170

safe deposit boxes, 173
sales
    of cars, 80–85
    of credit cards, 168
    of credit life insurance, 77–78
    of financial products, 64–68
    to married couples, 126–27
    See also retail sales
Salvation Army, 166
Sandwich Generation, 105
savings accounts
    in bankruptcy, 159
    for catastrophic expenses, 166
    contributions to, 24
    for education, 52–53, 159
    in family budget, 108
    function of, 49
    joint, 173
    rule of 72 for, 170
scholarships, for college, 167
seasonal influences on markets,
        134–35
SEC Rule 17a-3(17), 136
Securities and Exchange
        Commission (SEC), 135
Securities Investor Protection
        Corporation (SIPC), 57
security
    of credit cards, 97, 179
    of personal information, 54,
        62–63, 72, 79, 178–81
security freeze, 180
self-image, and financial plan,
        42–46
sellers
    bear markets and, 16
    market function of, 11
September 11, 2001 terrorist
        attacks, 131

shareholder value
    CEOs and, 141
    increasing, 119, 122
silver, as investment, 160
Small Business Administration
        (SBA), 165–66
Social Security, 184, 189
software
    for credit report monitoring,
        178–79
    for family budget, 103–104
    for financial portfolio review, 68
    for financial services, 58–59, 72
speculators, avoiding, 137
spending
    bankruptcy and, 162
    college students and, 168
    controlling, 41, 98, 143, 163
    having children and, 195
    vs. income, 119
    large-quantity purchases and,
        94–95
    marriage and, 186
    mortgage debt and, 86
    on needs vs. wants, 115, 176
    personal priorities and, 175
    See also expenses
spouse
    catastrophic expenses and, 165
    common financial goals with,
        188–89
    credit building and, 173–74
    employment and, 195
    family budget and, 105
    joint accounts with, 172–73, 186
    loss of, 117
    money problems with, 170–72
    shopping with vs. without,
        126–27

stamp collecting, 21
start-up businesses, 165, 201
stock market
    drivers of, 5–6
    function of, 4–5
    index funds and, 61
    infomercials about, 126
    price fluctuations in, 24
    systems for investing in, 6–7
stock options, 18, 69, 201
stock prices
    dollar cost averaging and, 24–25
    drivers of, 21, 131
    exit price and, 106
    gold prices and, 122
    in initial public offerings, 22
stock split, 13
stocks
    buying and selling of, 4–5, 51
    dividends from, 23–24
    in initial public offerings, 21–23
    as investments, 4, 17
    in mutual funds, 25
    researching, 61–62
    risk management with, 11–15,
        191
    teaching about, 20–21
    undervalued, 12
stop-loss orders
    executing, 106
    in risk management strategy, 70
store discounts, 93
stress, relieving, 112–13
student loans
    bankruptcy and, 158
    building credit and, 161
    paying for, 165, 167
subadvisors, 71
suitability rules, 135–36
sweepstakes scams, 192

tax planning, 200
taxes
    account consolidation and,
        54–55
    bankruptcy and, 158
    capital gains, 51
    on car sales, 81, 82
    custodial accounts and, 52
    on dividends, 23
    education savings accounts and,
        53
    loan points and, 88
    online record keeping for, 60, 72
    on real estate, 187
    retirement accounts and, 51–52,
        166, 184, 190
teaching financial concepts,
    109–110
television
    avoiding, 116
    financial programs on, 3, 20
time management, 116
Tony Robbins Wealth Mastery
    seminar, 146
traders
    financial awareness of, 73
    rules followed by, 129
    stock options and, 201
    stop orders and, 106
    stress on, 117
Transunion.com, 161
Treasury notes, 191
twelve months same as cash, 94

underwriters, in initial public
    offerings, 22–23
unemployment
    job hunting and, 183
    U.S. rate of (2008), xv
upside-down car loans, 82–83, 85

U.S. Department of Housing and
Urban Development (HUD),
128
U.S. Trustee Program, 159

value investing, 12
Vanguard, 28
Veribanc.com, 57
Vipers (Vanguard), 28
voting rights, and common stock,
22

The Wall Street Journal, 27
warehouse stores, 94
weddings, cost of, 185, 193
windfalls
gifts to others from, 199
protecting, 198–99

responsible allocation of,
197–98
withdrawals
from ATMs, 49, 50
early, from retirement accounts,
166
from IRAs, 52
from Roth IRAs, 52
from savings accounts, 49
work-at-home scams, 192

Yahoo!, 12–13
yield, from stock dividends, 23

zero down payment, on car sales,
81–82
zero percent APR, on credit cards,
76, 94

About the Authors

A. J. MONTE AND RICK SWOPE, also known as The Market Guys, have worked with hundreds of thousands of traders and investors in the United States and abroad. They give presentations around the world and host webinars and a blog on their website. Their podcast is consistently rated one of the top financial programs on the Web. They are the exclusive education providers for E*TRADE's five million accounts worldwide and host *Wealth & Wisdom,* a weekly financial show on WXEL PBS television in South Florida.

About the Type

This book was set in Times Roman, designed by Stanley Morrison specifically for *The Times* of London. The typeface was introduced in the newspaper in 1932. Times Roman had its greatest success in the United States as a book and commercial typeface, rather than one used in newspapers.